CW01020566

INSIDE *UTOPIA*

Visionary Interiors and
Futuristic Homes

gestalten

SHELLS
OF A HUMAN

THE FUTURE WAS BETTER THAN THE PRESENT AND THE HOME WAS THE CANVAS BY WHICH TO EXPRESS THAT.

Let us take a throne in a museum. As we approach it, we discover a canon of codes. Is it a secular or clerical furnishing? When exactly was it built? How highly esteemed was the person who sat upon it? And what do we know about concurrent manufacturing processes and tastes of the time? A throne is more than a functional item to sit on, and design in general reveals many different facets of life, all of which have co-existed since antiquity. But there are enduring core principles to be gathered: an affinity for decorative representation; a focus on new technologies; a quest for pureness at the same time as richness; a desire to refine the aesthetic form. In short, design is an expression of the ego.

Who am I, and what does society look like around me? There was a time when employing housemaids, cooks, and even chauffeurs was commonplace. Kitchens were isolated spaces in a house, dedicated to practical functions over impromptu social gatherings. Times have changed and so design has too. The kitchen has become the heart of the home. Examining the evolution of the living space and its expressive cues in the second half of the last century is illuminating. Because today our tastes revolve around that past more than ever, around an idea of it that never quite existed as imagined—just as the idea of a radical future back then never came true.

The 1950s were all about optimism, a postwar carpe diem. Family values abounded. A profitable job and simple pleasures like a nice glass of Scotch in the evening were enough. But after the world regained a certain kind of stability, a courageous nature came to the fore. It was a time for expressing one's personality—become a Playboy or It-Girl, celebrate your quirky mannerisms, and most importantly, dare to dream of a wild and radical future.

Not only did cars look like spaceships. Movies, books, and houses did too. The future was better than the present and the home was another canvas by which to express that. The leaders in designing that vision were the architects. Unlike today, architects were not bound to the outer walls and foundations of the home. They were the emperors of uncharted territory, and they created a complete work of art, from arranging the walls under a wave-shaped roof to carpeting the ceiling in op-art patterns. Interior design became something for artists, fashionistas, and designing dare devils—it became pop culture.

And today? From where we stand, one cannot help but notice that we have not gotten our flying cars—what we do have is a tweeting bird. The inner utopia did not eventuate. But design does not need to take root in reality; instead it should represent the best of us, and most of all inspire. The eclecticism that Carlo Mollino and others embodied in the 1950s came from time traveling into the history of design. Golden stucco above Louis XVI-armchairs in leopard prints alongside plastic chairs? On paper it sounds like design suicide. But its arrangement makes it coherent. It is less about singular ingredients and more about giving them fresh context in a new world—just as today. Keep in mind that brutalism was sneered at as a form of domestic architecture until its softness was discovered through a tropical twist. Now it is more modern than ever.

We can only mix up the many facets of design and give them a new lease on life by looking at where we began. So come and join our journey—INSIDE UTOPIA.

THE LEADERS IN DESIGNING THAT VISION WERE THE ARCHITECTS, EMPERORS OF UNCHARTED TERRITORY.

INSIDE UTOPIA

The conception of our living space changed radically during the last century. From art nouveau to rational modernism, the interior became a progressive tool reflecting our modern society.

The twentieth century encompasses 100 years of fast-paced innovation as our modern lifestyle came to be. Each new decade brought about completely new perspectives on how to behave within society. Architects and designers have always been at the forefront of these innovations, game changers in terms of how our daily lives are experienced.

As the twentieth century marched on, architecture and design replaced old-fashioned and bourgeois taste by celebrating new forms. Interior residential design, the epicenter of the architectural profession throughout the decades, became the conduit for experiments—where architects put their ideas into practice. The family became the perfect entity through which to explore the planning of the home, bringing about crucial developments in form and function. Our brief trip through the building styles of the 1900s to the 1980s will point to the radical changes that influenced the ever-evolving ways we engage with the modern world.

The flamboyant and decorative art-nouveau style in the first years of the last century ushered in completely new ideas of architecture and living. After short periods of expressionism, futurism, and other decorative derivatives, the ideology of modernism rose to power. Modernism was born from the desire to create a new universe of architecture and design that would liberate the individual and create an equitable social environment. The movement was a utopian, poetic materialization for the modern age, a

time when humans first drove a car, flew an airplane, and circled the globe by boat. Technology was a central inspiration for designers and architects, transferring the language of the industrial age to furniture and buildings.

In 1919, Walter Gropius founded Bauhaus in Weimar as an art-school prototype, where artists would be educated to collaborate with industry. A few years later, Le Corbusier wrote his *Five Points of Modern Architecture*, a groundbreaking essay on the essentials for a healthy modern home. And Frank Lloyd Wright's conception of open-plan living, later mastered by Mies van der Rohe, was central to the vision of the time.

The architects of modernism had a new mantra: form follows function. The visual reality of their houses turned out quite differently, much of the architecture too radical for the mainstream. While society was not quite prepared to live in such forms, architects of the 1920s and 1930s saw themselves as scientists of sorts, in service of creating a better world through design. According to Le Corbusier, a house was a "machine for living." These projects shed light on a free-spirited artistic mind rather than manifesting as practical dwellings for daily living.

Despite its paradoxes, controversies, and fails, the interwar period was a laboratory from which the many styles of the postwar period bubbled up. Frank Lloyd Wright and Eero Saarinen pioneered organic architecture; Le Corbusier brutalism; Mies van der Rohe transparent Californian modernism; and art deco designers

BY ADAM ŠTĚCH

eclectic decorative design of the 1950s and 1960s, as an alternative to radical modernism.

JOY OF LIVING: MIDCENTURY MODERN

PP. 8–95

The optimistic atmosphere of the postwar period was echoed in midcentury design and architecture. Radical interwar modernism was folded into everyday living with softer, more organic forms. An international style of architecture dominated by flat roofs, open spaces, floor-to-ceiling windows, and material sensitivity suddenly spread out across the world. Many countries contributed to this design-oriented way of living through their regional applications.

The United States led the way as the economic boom brought endless possibilities for the middle class. While a modernist house in the 1930s was a privilege reserved for the elites, in the 1950s it symbolized a prosperous middle-class family. California became the center of the architectural avant-garde. Rigid modernism was adapted to the mild climate, and architects such as Charles and Ray Eames, Pierre Koenig and A. Quincy Jones were swept into stardom as the Californian residential phenomenon took off.

But light transparent modernism made a splash in Europe too, primarily in Scandinavia, where architects connected the established aesthetics with an unmistakable sense for materials. Danish architects of the 1950s such as Arne Jacobsen or Karen and Ebbe Clemmensen celebrated the house as a personalized and well-crafted space.

Italy also experienced a boom in its economy in the 1950s, and design and architecture within the culture flourished, as it still does today. Architects such as Ico Parisi and put Italy on the international modernist map with their elegance and decorative flair. The symbiosis of simple, modern structures and colorful decoration is exemplified in Gio Ponti's residential masterpiece of the last century, Villa Planchart in Caracas.

Midcentury modernism was truly global. European immigrants in Latin America, Africa, and Australia made significant contributions within these tropical environments. Glazed residences, open toward nature, gave fresh air to modern ways of living.

— *Elrod House* by John Lautner, pp. 60–63

ALTERNATIVE TO MODERNISM: INTERIOR DECORATION

PP. 96–143

The clean and geometric forms of midcentury modernism stand in contrast to the glamorous and eccentric style of interior designers, who flamboyantly rode the wave of eclecticism. Italian Carlo Mollino took from the eclectic forms of baroque or art nouveau and created his own colorful take on modernism, as did American set designer Tony Duquette. Magic, frivolity, and exotic sources of inspiration were familiar to the masters of the decorative movement, including Italian designer Piero Fornasetti.

While designers like Jean Prouvé or Charlotte Perriand championed standardized environments and mass-produced goods in the name of modernism, other French designers were influenced by the rich heritage of master carpenters, or ébéniste, and the decorative language of modern art deco.

INTERIOR PSYCHEDELIA: ORGANICISM, SPACE AGE, AND RADICAL DESIGN

PP. 144–229

The spiritual and utopian visions of the 1950s and 1960s imagined the living space as an experimental environment, where anything and everything is possible. The clean lines of fine midcentury modernism mutated into unexpected creative imagery. The residential interior became a playground for both architects and their clients.

In the U.S., organic architecture was well received during the 1940s and 1950s thanks to icons like Frank Lloyd Wright and John Lautner, whose designs were still rooted in the strict beginnings of modernism. But it was the self-taught Bruce Goff who pioneered an individualism in residential solutions, his experimental structures made of raw materials highlighted by unconventional decorations. His breathtaking spaces, similar to the architecture of Herb Greene and Bart Prince, established a whole new experience for the homeowner.

— *Palais Bulles* by Antti Lovag,
   pp. 220–225

Across the ocean, the decorative scene in the U.S. from the 1950s to 1970s was also burgeoning. Designers like Vladimir Kagan designed furniture pieces that could be viewed as individual works of art, while George Nelson and Charles Eames created famous industrially produced goods. The studio furniture movement, a rich chapter in American interior design, was pioneered by Wharton Esherick and later perfected by Georges Nakashima with Paul Evans and Wendell Castle.

— *Dawnridge* by Tony Duquette,
   pp. 112–119

The European decorators scene bordered quite closely on fine arts. In 1970s France, interior objects doubled as autonomous forms of artistic expression, as we can see in the brilliant design work of François-Xavier and Claude Lalanne, and Jacques Duval-Brasseur, among others.

INTRODUCTION   BY ADAM ŠTĚCH

The active experience was crucial in the work of 1960s space-age designers. Radical Italians such as Ettore Sottsass or the Danish Verner Panton envisioned the home as a compact organic environment created of built-in furniture, lighting, and other interior objects. Designers evoked a free-spirited interior environment with no conventional pieces of furniture in sight. Plastics were integrated into the projects of Charles Deaton in Colorado or the furniture and houses of Wolfgang Feierbach.

These radical architectural visions in 1960s and 1970s Europe took a sculptural approach, connecting natural organic forms by using concrete. Architects such as Claude Häusermann-Costy or Daniel Grataloup used extensively sprayed concrete to build bubble-like structures, where living spaces morphed into modernist utopian caves.

ROUGHNESS OF FORM: BRUTALISM

PP. 230–299

Brutalism flourished from the 1950s to the 1970s, succeeding the modernist movements of the early twentieth century. The term describes the raw appearance of materials, mainly exposed concrete, with Le Corbusier's later material poetry rooted in these concrete properties.

The style was manifested in public buildings at the start, the cold, rough aesthetic of exposed concrete rarely translating to the domestic realm. In Europe, an experimental group of Swiss architects in the 1960s and those in Belgium masterfully applied the brutalist language to domestic projects. Juliaan Lampens was among the most interesting of these innovators. He built several radical houses made of concrete, embracing new concepts of community living within the family over old-fashioned private hierarchies.

Brutalism as a style of residential architecture was well received in tropical regions, where concrete worked as a great cooling agent against the hot climate. In São Paulo, Paulo Mendes da Rocha, João Batista Vilanova

Artigas, Eduardo Longo, and others used exposed concrete to create the influential Paulista school of architecture. They built bunker-like residential structures with refined interior solutions. Mexican architect Luis Barragán also worked with concrete, his colorful designs building on classic brutalism, but adding a poetic legacy out of the monumentality of modernist architecture.

Brutalism was the last movement of the International Style and the last victory of modernism. During the

— *Leme House* by Paolo Mendes da Rocha, pp. 258–265

1960s, 1970s, and 1980s, many fundamental principles from these movements would still inform a new breed of architecture and design. But modernism as an ideology would come under criticism, replaced by the ironic and entertaining language of postmodernism.

REFLECTING THE ARTISTIC ECHO OF AN OPTIMISTIC ATMOSPHERE

— *Elrod House* by John Lautner,
pp. 60–63

Stahl House

Pierre Koenig built a cultural icon with the Stahl House. An emblematic project of the Case Study House program, it defined a new way of life in postwar California.

Architect: Pierre Koenig
Location: Los Angeles, CA, USA
Completion date: 1957

There is no house more iconic of the California modern movement than the Stahl House, the finest work of architect Pierre Koenig. Built as Case Study House #22, the L-shaped, one-story residence in the Hollywood Hills of Los Angeles is the finest example of a new type of postwar modernist style. The Case Study House program, an influential project curated by John Entenza of *Arts & Architecture* magazine, set a new standard for open-space, democratic postwar living.

Buck and Charlotte Stahl purchased a small lot above Sunset Boulevard in 1954. For years, they spent every weekend working on the steep plot to prepare it for their dream house. In 1957, they hired Pierre Koenig to realize their plans, and two years later his project became part of the Case Study House program. Koenig created the two-bedroom, 200-square-meter residence as a true testament to modernist architecture. Constructed of glass and steel, the residence opens its interior to the endless urban sprawl of Los Angeles. Lightweight steel supports the sun-filled pavilion-like structure with nearly transparent floor-to-ceiling glass walls. The central living room is wide open, sectioned only by a central kitchen module. The architect

fig. a   fig. b (opposite page)

fig. a: The kitchen is composed of built-in cabinets and lighting modules, dividing the open-plan living space.

fig. b: The L-shaped layout of the Stahl House is complemented by the pool and spectacular view over Los Angeles.

envisioned the Californian dream of open living, where interior and exterior borders are blurred.

The Stahl House is probably the most popular of all the Case Study Houses. It helps that celebrated photographer Julius Shulman created some of the most iconic photos in the history of architecture when shooting the home. He brought to light sunny days by the pool and atmospheric evenings with women dressed in beautiful gowns—the American dream come true. Both the photos and the home's design celebrate a glamorous lifestyle bathed in 1950s modernism. The house is now a national landmark open to the public. (STE)

Built as Case Study House 22, this L-shaped, one-story residence in the Hollywood Hills of Los Angeles is the finest example of a new type of postwar modernist style.

fig. c

PIERRE KOENIG

STAHL HOUSE

fig. d

fig. c, d, e, & f: Stahl
House became a prototype
of Californian modern
architecture, celebrated
in photos by famous
American photographer
Julius Shulman.

fig. e   fig. f (following double page)

Miller House

Architect: Eero Saarinen
Location: Columbus, IN, USA
Completion date: 1953

Eero Saarinen shows off his unequaled aptitude for adapting the revolutionary design ideas of his age to match the expectations of prestigious clients.

Symmetry was problematic to many architects of this period, not simply because it was a trope of a bygone era, but because an overly conceptual plan ran counter to the concept of form following function. Symmetrical houses had a hierarchy of

The three-by-three plan is subtly expressed in a grid pattern of skylights supported by steel columns. Generally, the relationship between the rooms is free and open, with a dining space off the main space—complete with Saarinen's own Tulip chairs.

The strength of the house is not only in the plan, which draws upon historic precedents without repeating them; it is also in the astonishing interiors by Alexander Girard, particularly the bespoke textiles created for the curtains and drapes. The lounge pit is not just a formal exercise in creating inbuilt furniture, but an opportunity for Girard to fill it with a sumptuous array of patterns and textures in textile form.

Bedrooms occupy the corners of the single-floor house. This allows the homeowner and guests continual exposure to the astonishing gardens, as two sides of each bedroom are given over to floor-to-ceiling glazing. Elsewhere in the house, such as the dining room, the same glazing can be fully withdrawn so as to experience a direct relationship with Daniel Urban Kiley's formal, Japanese-inspired garden. (ABR)

fig. a

fig. a: There are few better settings for Eero Saarinen's own Tulip chairs that he created for Knoll in the 1950s.

fig. b: Saarinen faces down the predilection amongst his contemporaries for placing the entrance off centre.

fig. c & d: The inbuilt rectilinear cabinet and the square sunken sofa pit offset the more extravagant tastes of the client.

rooms that prescribed a function to the form: the wrong way around in the eyes of the modernists. Saarinen had no such problem with symmetry, but at the Miller House he used it in a pioneering way to create a three-by-three grid of spaces. This put the fireplace and a lounge pit at the heart of the house—almost like a primitive hut. He then arranged the other rooms around it. It works to spectacular effect. Commissioned by industrialist, church leader, and civil rights activist J. Irwin Miller and his wife, the Miller House is considered a proposition as to the future of the house, in a similar way as the Farnsworth House was to Mies van der Rohe or the Glass House to Philip Johnson.

fig. b   fig. c (opposite page)   fig. d (following double page)

fig. e

fig. e: Simple corner bedrooms with floor to ceiling glazing offer views out on to the ordered landscaping.

fig. f: Initially designated by architect Eero Saarinen to be the playroom, this later became Xenia Miller's office.

fig. g: Alexander Girard created bespoke carpets. In one instance the plan of the house is used as a motif.

fig. f

fig. 8

At the Miller House, Saarinen used symmetry in a pioneering way to create a three-by-three grid of spaces. This put the fireplace and a lounge pit at the heart of the house—almost like a primitive hut.

The strength of the house is not only in the plan, which
draws upon historic precedents without repeating them; it is also
in the astonishing interiors by Alexander Girard, particularly the
bespoke textiles created for the curtains and drapes.

fig. i

fig. h, i, & j: Girard
worked on the house
for over 15 years,
adorning its windows
with his fabrics and
adapting it to change.

Eames House

Architect: Charles & Ray Eames
Location: Pacific Palisades, CA, USA
Completion date: 1949

The modern designer's interior non pareil. The Eames House manages to showcase the designers' furniture in a way that brings them to vibrant life.

fig. a

fig. a: The jazzy arrangement of partition and glazing turns a rectangular volume into a building with pizazz.

fig. b: Despite the simplicity of the structure, internally the building is blessed with discrete areas like the kitchen.

fig. c: The single structural innovation on the interior is a mezzanine, which creates a cosy seating area beneath.

fig. d: The interior of the house is a joyful retort to the accusation that modernism is resistant to color.

fig. e: Charles Eames in the studio. The house is adorned with a range of complimentary modernist and ethnic art.

Although it became Charles and Ray Eames's own home, the Eames House began life as number #8 of the Case Study Houses. This unparalleled project sought to explore innovations in residential architecture in the United States and, unbelievable as it may seem today, was sponsored by a magazine, *Arts & Architecture*. The publication commissioned major architects of the day, including Richard Neutra, Pierre Koenig, and A. Quincy Jones, to draw and then build cheap exemplars of homes for veterans returning from the Second World War, as well as for a new generation of immigrants in the western U.S. The house was to be made of prefabricated materials that would be harmonious with the existing site, and easy to build from modern materials. This site sits atop a 15-meter cliff with a view out to the Pacific Ocean. A steep incline to the west creates a natural retaining wall. The site is flat, although it has been lined by another concrete retaining wall beneath the slope. This device structurally ties together the two double-height, steel-framed boxes separated by a courtyard. One of the boxes was designed as a home, the other a studio. The interior of the house is warm and comforting, with wooden parquet flooring and wooden staircases

floating between floors. In contrast to the steel frame of the structure, the infilled paneling is made from a wide range of solid and transparent colored panels, which create a shifting mosaic of light across the interior throughout the day. Planted along the side of the house is a row of eucalyptus trees that provides shade and introduces greenery into close proximity. Rooms flow into one another across the plan, but also into double-height spaces. In dissolving boundaries between spaces, the house permits an almost endless interplay between different materials—the modern, synthetic, and the natural—showing that modernism can be eclectic as well as refined. (ABR)

fig. b   fig. c (opposite page)

The house was to be made of prefabricated materials that would be harmonious with the existing site and easy to build from modern materials.

26   CHARLES & RAY EAMES   EAMES HOUSE

Gertler House

An elevated sculpture in redwood with a tree at its very heart. This stunning structure married timeless material with modern design principles.

Architect: Ray Kappe
Location: Santa Monica, CA, USA
Completion date: 1970

Of the more than 100 houses that Ray Kappe designed throughout his career, the ones he designed in Rustic Canyon in Los Angeles are his most interesting and impressive; they define an image of easy Californian luxury that lingers on in the movies and box-set series of today. Elsewhere, the home he built for himself wraps around the slope in the Palisades. The Gertler House, however, sits on relatively flat ground as one approaches it. The house itself is effectively composed of a number of steel boxes clad in redwood and suspended several meters above the ground, which slopes away steeply from front to rear on ten redwood towers. Although the façade of the house facing the entrance is wrapped in the warm, richly textured redwood that dominates the natural woodlands of California, it is also flooded with light from skylights and clerestories. As one moves into the house, even more of the singular light of southern California floods into the room from the glazed walls to the rear. From the central atrium space, all the rooms of the main floor effectively unfold and are in view at once. They offer a series of functions: an open kitchen, a formal dining space, and a living and family room framed by walls of glass and redwood. The two bedrooms are shuttered in redwood to a greater degree to offer privacy. All the spaces for entertaining are adjoined by exterior decks, which provide both intimate, up-close views of nature and long-distance ones. Space above the expansive ground floor allows for more bedrooms, and a lower level nestling within the structure, supporting the main-floor area, provides a private bedroom suite with family rooms. In this house, Kappe, who founded the Southern California Institute of Architecture, pushed forward the typology of modernist homes in the west of the U.S. His design exemplifies a greater understanding of the need for occasional privacy in the home, with an appreciation for natural materials. Bucking the use of steel and concrete, his choice of wood suited the growing environmental concerns in architecture, which took hold in the Sunshine State of the 1960s far earlier than in the rest of the world. (ABR)

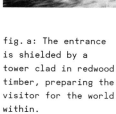

fig. a   fig. b (opposite page)

fig. a: The entrance is shielded by a tower clad in redwood timber, preparing the visitor for the world within.

fig. b: Saarinen's Womb chair strikes the perfect note, in the middle of the home amongst traditional furniture.

In this house, Kappe pushed forward the typology of modernist homes. His design exemplifies a greater understanding of the need for occasional privacy in the home, with an appreciation for natural materials.

fig. c

fig. d

fig. c, d, & e: The
interior is a series
of platforms on the
same raised level,
visible to each other
and to the exterior.

fig. e

Smalley House

Architect: A. Quincy Jones
Location: Los Angeles, CA, USA
Completion date: 1974

A high-pitched, cathedral-like atrium dominates this dwelling in Los Angeles, challenging preconceived ideas of conventional domestic design.

fig. a

fig. a & b: The home's exterior belies its interior makeup. From various angles, the building appears to be single-story.

fig. c: The triple-height atrium: What better furniture for this mid-1970s space than Warren Platner's wire lounge chairs for Knoll?

fig. d: Looking down into the living room from the entrance of the house toward the glazed double-height end wall.

fig. e: The bedroom. The raked ceiling in the bedroom is clad in Douglas fir, as are many of the walls throughout the house.

Architect A. Quincy Jones, with his colleague Frederick Emmons, successfully designed more than 5,000 high-quality tract homes across California. Though arguably best known for these houses, Jones was as capable in designing stunning larger homes, exemplified in the Smalley House. Highly valued, the house, which he designed late in his career, could almost be called a villa. Originally designed for Marvin and Sandy Smalley, it was purchased in 2006 by philanthropist and art curator Shula Nazarian.

Rather than being a departure from his work on small family homes, the Smalley House, which Jones designed alone, exhibits all the tropes of his previous projects. Like his earlier tract houses, it incorporates a usable atrium with high-pitched ceilings. The post-and-beam construction has been highly refined. It still acts not only as a structural principle that underpins the building but also as an aesthetic framing device for the natural world. The Smalley House enshrines Jones's reputation for designing from the inside out. But here his strategy receives a special twist: The visitor is introduced to the main body of the house, which

runs perpendicular to it at a raised level. The atrium, however, drops away in front of the visitor toward the garden. A planted internal garden invites the visitor onward, the exotic flora of California flowing down into the living room. In addition, a textured cedar wall begins near the front door and, serving as a spine to the house, draws the visitor onwards to the sunken secondary space. The arrival into the living space is dominated by a large table in front of a double-height window that looks out onto the garden. A corridor off the foyer and dining room leads to a wing with the kitchen, family, and children's rooms.

It is a subtle but ingenious series of interplays between the outdoor and indoor, which make for an incredible promenade. The building was refurbished in the twenty-first century to accommodate the owner's current lifestyle. The Los Angeles practice Scrafano Architects restored much of the original design, including patient restoration work on the unique river rock pebble flooring, the sumptuously lined Douglas-fir-clad ceilings, and the huge brick fireplace and hearth. (ABR)

fig. b fig. c (opposite page)

fig. d (opposite page)   fig. e

The Smalley House enshrines Jones's reputation for designing
from the inside out. A planted internal garden invites the visitor onward, the exotic flora of California flowing down into the living room.

Tempo House

Architect: Ray Kappe
Location: Los Angeles, CA, USA
Completion date: 1959

The glamour of Hollywood is never far away from Californian modernism and particularly so with this sumptuous, sundrenched, and pool-dominated house.

fig. a

fig. a & c: The interior is dominated by the circular form of the pool which is accentuated by supporting columns.

fig. b: The house is protected from the road on the opposite side to the pool by a screen of besser block.

fig. b   fig. c (opposite page)

The client is always in charge. While Ray Kappe was brought up among the pure principles of Californian modernism—his own junior high school, Emerson Middle School, was designed by Richard Neutra, and he built nearly 100 homes in the style from the 1950s onward—he worked for private clients as well. Los Angeles is not always a place where honesty to materials, one of the tenets of modernism, is respected. It is a place of high theater, and with the Tempo House, Kappe rises to the occasion. Eschewing the simple metal piloti or I-beam columns used by modernist architects throughout the world, Kappe used a palisade of columns to create the dominant aesthetic feature of the property. Although in his early days Kappe had worked with the firm Anshen & Allen on making post-and-beam constructions organized around a single module, in later life he was not averse to adapting to the times. Eschewing the strict perpendicular lines of the post-and-beam construction, Kappe designed a huge circular swimming pool for the Tempo House, its roof supported by a series of simple stone clad columns. Kappe kept the classical references to a minimum; he did not give his columns any capitals, and he was able to adapt his commitment to the spirit of the age with its open-plan living. In a nice twist, the plan of the house picks up on the pool's circular form. Still dedicated to the rational and intuitive in the manner of a good modernist, the living spaces are an enclosed version of the series of columns around the pool. As the house moves closer to the road, away from the public space of the pool that looks out across on neighbors, it becomes more secluded. Kappe came to adapt his architectural approach in many different ways, while also becoming founding director of SCI-Arc, the Southern California Institute of Architecture. SCI-Arc became internationally recognized for its open, experimental attitude and teaching methods. But as postmodernism flourished, SCI-Arc moved away from Kappe's interests in favor of more irrational and esoteric approaches to design. He left his post as director in 1987. (ABR)

Kappe kept the classical references to a minimum; he did not give his columns any capitals, and he was able to adapt his commitment to the spirit of the age with its open-plan living.

fig. d: The sitting room with floor to ceiling glazing faces out on to the garden and is full of modernist furniture.

fig. e: Screened by the besser block wall beyond, the bedroom is able to be fully open to the garden.

fig. f: The kitchen stands at the heart of the house and boasts a counter that almost surrounds it on four sides.

fig. e

fig. f

Kappe House

Built over a small creek in Los Angeles's Rustic Canyon, the home of Californian architect Ray Kappe is a structural wonder that floats above the wild, steep landscape.

Architect: Ray Kappe
Location: Los Angeles, CA, USA
Completion date: 1967

Born in 1927, Ray Kappe belongs to the heroic generation of Californian architects who gave the movement an exceptional name beginning in the 1940s. His contributions to the Californian architectural vocabulary of stunning spaces, large glass surfaces, and original construction solutions are of the same quality as his more famous contemporaries.

The architect, who co-founded the prestigious Southern California Institute of Architecture (SCI-Arc), became a master of spacious residential builds during the 1950s, focusing his efforts on private homes. Among the 100 houses he designed during his extensive career, his own residence is his masterpiece. Designed for himself and his wife Shelly and built in 1967, the structure shows his affinity for the sleek and geometric forms of Californian modernism, as well as a considered harmony with its natural surroundings, as championed by Frank Lloyd Wright.

"Maybe the greatest house in all of Southern California," said Stephen Kanner, former president of the American Institute of Architects' Los Angeles chapter, in an

fig. a   fig. b (opposite page)

fig. a: The house of Ray Kappe is surrounded by lush vegetation. Today, his vintage Jaguar can still be seen parked outside.

interview about this marvel of form and space. The structure is built over a steep hill, elevated on seven rectangular concrete pillars that are tucked into the ground. Kappe designed these pillars to bear horizontal platforms of varied heights, creating an experiential indoor space.

The house opens into a complex interior landscape, where each area has a different height and only a few steps dividing one from another. The most spectacular area is the main living room with built-in seating and a large glass window, which allows for a union with nature. (STE)

The structure of the house is built over a steep hill, elevated on the seven rectangular concrete pillars tucked into the ground.

fig. c

RAY KAPPE

KAPPE HOUSE

fig. b, c, d, & e:
Kappe succeeded in
connecting the geo-
metric modernist
rationale with the
natural materials and
organic appearance
of the living space.

Block Island House

Architect: Jens Risom
Location: Block Island, RI, USA
Completion date: 1965

Perched upon a sparsely populated island just 20 kilometers off the New England coast, Jens Risom's once-humble prefab has become a 1960s timewarp.

fig. a

fig. a & b: Risom's prefab sits within a low, dry-stone-wall compound. Its glazed north-facing end looks straight out to sea.

fig. c: Most of the downstairs area is a double-height space with open-plan kitchen, dining room, and living room. To the rear of the house are bedrooms and a bathroom. Upstairs, a loft space provides rooms for the children.

In 1941, the late Jens Risom teamed up with Hans Knoll to create the Hans Knoll Furniture Company. It should come as no surprise, therefore, to find that the "timewarp" furniture filling the rooms of this Block Island Retreat are pieces that Risom designed himself—some of them prototypes that never made it onto the showroom floor.

Risom bought the prefab for 20,700 dollars half a century ago but, of course, this is not any old off-the-peg model. Produced by a Massachusetts-based company called Stanmar, this is a prefab that Risom customized to suit his own design-conscious requirements. In doing so, he turned it into an architectural icon for decades to come. The first thing Risom did was to replace the north-facing gable end with an entire wall of glass. Not only did this flood the interior with ever-changing daylight, but it allowed him to have a main living space with ceiling heights of six meters. Crucially, from an aesthetic point of view, Risom clad the exterior of the prefab in cedar shingles rather than the standard-model asphalt ones. Over the years, the shingles have mellowed—silvering as a result of natural

weathering—giving the building an almost vernacular feel to it. Inside, the interior design has a modular feel to it, in keeping with much midcentury style. The furniture is simple and geometric in outline; the bare oak and teak wood of the furniture and open kitchen shelving mirrors the exposed wood of the prefab's timber frame. Colors are those inspired by nature—orange, green, yellow—but with a 60s zing. (SOU)

fig. b   fig. c (opposite page)

44

"I always knew that I wanted to design, but only
if I could create products over which I had total control."
Jens Risom

fig. e

fig. d & e: The sofa
in the living room
is a prototype for a
sofabed that never
went into production.
The support for the
seat cushions slides
out to make a double-
bed platform.

fig. f: This button-
back rocking chair
dates from 2008 and is
also a Risom design.
It has midcentury
century style and has
been upholstered in
a 60s-looking orange
fabric.

fig. f

Nakashima House

Architect: Georges Nakashima
Location: New Hope, PA, USA
Completion date: 1954–1975

Versatile American designer and craftsman George Nakashima connected masterful carpentry, a sculptural sensibility, and spirituality in his exceptional designs. His New Hope studio, still open to the public today, embodies this work.

fig. a

fig. a & g: Kevin, the son of George Nakashima, relaxes in the Conoid Studio, the main building on Nakashima's New Hope property.

fig. b: Nakashima designed only a few buildings. But every design demonstrates his creative energy and spectacular solutions, as with the vault of the Conoid Studio.

fig. c: Interior of the Minguren Museum, the last structure completed on the property in 1967.

For more than half a century George Nakashima created unique sculptural furniture. With a great respect for the natural qualities of wood, he crafted his designs from his large estate in New Hope, Pennsylvania. To this day, his remarkable legacy lives on through his family, who produces fine artisan furniture under his trademarked name. It is a name that has come to be one of the most respected in the history of modern American decorative arts. Nakashima was born in 1905 in Spokane, Washington, and decided early on that he would study architecture. He attended the University of Washington and in 1931 received a master's degree from M.I.T. He then settled in Japan and joined the Tokyo studio of famous architect Antonin Raymond. During the war, Nakashima returned to the United States, but was then forced into a Japanese internment camp for some time. In 1946, the architect bought a large plot of land in New Hope and began building his dream.

New Hope was a lively artistic community at that time. Neighbors included Phillip Lloyd Powell and Paul Evans, other leaders of the postwar studio furniture movement. Because of Nakashima's increasing profile during the 1950s, he built several other structures including a showroom, studio, arts building, and storage facility for wood. The woodworker completed

his Conoid Studio with its signature semicircular roof in 1956. Inside, he designed a series of furniture solitaires named Conoid. The series included a cantilevered chair that later became one of his most famous and best-selling pieces. In 1967, Nakashima completed one of the last buildings on this extensive property; the Minguren Museum, an arts building, was the culmination of all his ambitions as an architect. The exterior of the building is decorated with an abstract mosaic painting by Ben Shahn. Currently, the property of George Nakashima is listed on the U.S. National Register of Historic Places and still plays a key role in the production of his eponymous company. (STE)

fig. b   fig. c (opposite page)

fig. d: The Minguren Museum was used by Nakashima and his collaborators for family celebrations and special events.

fig. e: The rough organic ceiling of the Conoid Studio fits with the stone masonry and beauty of Nakashima's wood furniture.

fig. f: The Studio is furnished with cozy seating areas, such as this one with a built-in sofa and Nakashima-designed carpet.

fig. d

fig. e

fig. f

Nakashima dedicated his entire life to designing and producing a limited release of custom furniture, individual pieces of art that earned him a place at the forefront of the studio furniture movement.

fig. 8

51

Frey House II

Architect: Albert Frey
Location: Palm Springs, CA, USA
Completion date: 1948

Albert Frey's rudimentary house, built in vernacular materials, creates a homely aspect from which to contemplate the most epic of views—equal to any Western.

Few architects can claim to have influenced the aesthetic of an entire American city in the way that Swiss-born Albert Frey did. His second residence in his adopted home of Palm Springs is considered of such historical significance to the city that it is now in the care of the Palm Springs Art Museum. This is not because of its worth alone, but because the itinerant Frey put down roots in the city after the Second World War and built a number of local landmarks such as the Palm Springs City Hall.

arrangement. Frey studied the angle of the sun throughout the seasons in order to choose the best position for the house to sit within the rocky crags, erecting a concrete block plinth at just the right angle to build on. At only 75 square meters, the small home is made from simple materials. A flat corrugated-aluminum roof shades the interior from the harsh summer sun. Elsewhere, the large windows show off incredible views of Palm Springs and the mountains. The house relies deeply on its relationship with nature. The lower level features the living spaces: living room, master bedroom, and kitchen. Above sits a dining/work table and the bathroom. Frey added an additional guest bedroom in 1967. The stlye of the interior is tinged with the desert. The yellow Encilla flowers that bloom each spring in the desert are referenced in the curtains, while the ceiling is painted blue. References to the natural landscape are not entirely metaphorical: a large boulder protrudes into the design, functioning as a divider between the bedroom—open on two sides to views of the city—and the living room, beyond which lies the pool. Like the waterfall in Frank Lloyd Wright's Fallingwater house, Frey masterfully uses ultra-modern means to showcase an intimate way of living with and respecting nature. (ABR)

fig. a

fig. a: An extant rock provides a structural support to the second home Frey built for himself in Palm Springs.

fig. b & c: Internally the rocks act as partitions: a means of delineating different uses of the otherwise open plan.

In Frey's house lies the architectural DNA of the city. With a simple steel structure, it is clad in glass and painted corrugated metal. In formal terms, the home is one of the earliest and strongest testaments to modernism as a movement not just suitable for civic infrastructure and tall office blocks in Manhattan, but also for an intimate way of living with nature. Here, even in an extreme climate, the design works among the mountainous desert terrain with which Frey had become enamored.

Constructed of cheap materials including cinder blocks, aluminum, and glass, the Frey House II in Palm Springs is couched within the rock. But make no mistake, this is not a haphazard

fig. b   fig. c (opposite page)

fig. d: Seating is embedded into the concrete plinth upon which the house sits. The pool is embedded into the hill.

fig. e: The house's internal arrangement makes use of the differences in the pre-existing terrain levels.

fig. f & g: Extra charm derives from the ingenious way bespoke fixtures and fittings have been incorporated.

fig. f

fig. g

Mirman House Arcadia

Architects: Buff, Straub, and Hensman
Location: Arcadia, CA, USA
Completion date: 1958

This elegant house is not just an essay on how to build in the modernist manner in a hot climate, but how to live there.

fig. a

fig. a: A view from within the garden room to the exterior: Here, pool side living has become a fine art.

fig. b & c: As while playing shuffle board. The landscaping provides an informal setting where the generations mingle.

We can study the theory behind the revolutionary ideas of the modernists and the houses they built in California and the western United States in the 1950s and 1960s. But it is in the photographs shot by the great Julius Shulman that we really learn about these homes. While his pictures of works by Lautner, Neutra, and others are stunning, those of the Mirman House are exceptional. Here we have a visual manifesto for what the great landscape designer of the time, Garrett Eckbo, called a "landscape for living." The photographs invariably feature the figures of the family, at play or relaxing, both inside and outside the house. They convey the idea to the viewer that the gardens and the interiors are continuous. But they also illustrate that the exterior was zoned for specific kinds of activity: here is where one plays deck shuffleboard; here is the pool. A series of spaces is determined not by a hierarchy, or even typology, but by function. The Mirman House

exemplifies a new, relaxed, and very Californian approach to domestic architecture. Gone are walls on which to hang pictures or furniture that inhibits either movement or the view. Decking appears both inside and outside the house, and a pavilion for the sole purpose of relaxation mediates the two. In addition, a long canopy alongside it further blurs the distinction between the indoor and out. Built-in seating is low slung, allowing an unobstructed view straight through the house from one exterior to the other. All other furnishings are temporary, such as stools and cushions. Little distinction is made between space for gatherings and space for solitude. More than any of his pictures, Julius Shulman's work at the Mirman house, in which he choreographed the owners at play and at rest in their new steel garden pavilion, captured the ideas behind a dawning age. These images promoted the values of the modernist design ethos to a new set of clients with large amounts of disposable income and a desire to enjoy the Californian climate and the lifestyles that it could support. (ABR)

fig. b   fig. c (opposite page)

A series of spaces is determined not by a hierarchy, or even typology, but by function. The Mirman House exemplifies a new, relaxed, and very Californian approach to domestic architecture.

fig. d

BUFF, STRAUB, AND HENSMAN

MIRMAN HOUSE ARCADIA

fig. d & e: Wooden platforms create a visual continuity between the interior and the exterior of the garden room.

fig. f: The garden room's purpose was to provide for leisure. Here, piano and TV are encased in bespoke cabinets.

Elrod House

Architect: John Lautner
Location: Palm Springs, CA, USA
Completion date: 1968

Few interiors have been better used as a set in a spy thriller than the Elrod House.
Showcasing its combination of grandeur and superb detailing.

fig. a

fig. a & c: The concrete dome is an astonishing piece of engineering and the building's main architectural gesture.

fig. b: The terrace and the pool wrap around the circular house, providing further means to enjoy the view.

fig. d: Underneath the dramatic upper rooms are a series of intimate spaces such as this very groovy sitting room.

Elrod House is famous for its starring role as a set in the James Bond film *Diamonds Are Forever*. Murray Grigor's film about John Lautner not only begins with the shot of Sean Connery passing through the superbly finished granite-and-glass entrance, but proceeds with the actor narrating his experience of arriving in the house and being stunned by it. Less is known of the Elrod House's origins. The client for this breathtaking residence was Arthur Elrod, an interior designer who effectively defined the "look" for the Palm Springs midcentury-modern house. This extravagant, sculptural home provided him with an opportunity to show off his skills to the extreme. It seems strange to describe Lautner's design as restrained, but effectively he reserves his love of the monumental gesture for an 18-meter vaulted dome ceiling. It is constructed from nine concrete petals between nine clerestory windows, flooding the room with natural light.

Elrod arrived in the early 1950s and in setting up his company, Arthur Elrod and Associates, he swept aside the formal French Provincial style for sensual steel-framed furniture. This provided a new informality for the Hollywood set who came to town to party. The main circular space of the home gave Elrod ample opportunity to work his magic by using serpentine banquets and circular coffee tables—signatures of his style. The effect of this luxuriously curved furniture is heightened by the way in which the bare rock was left exposed by the architect. The building mimics Elrod's favored designs, which entailed wrapping around a larger form—the rock—in an organic fashion. (ABR)

fig. b   fig. c (opposite page)   fig. d (following double page)

Segel House

Architect: John Lautner
Location: Los Angeles, CA, USA
Completion date: 1979

Rising up from the golden sands of Carbon Beach in Malibu, the Segel Residence is the epitome of American midcentury-modern design.

fig. a

fig. a & c: Lautner uses wood structurally in his designs, but also decoratively to create repeating patterns and organic forms.

fig. b: A view of the house from the beach demonstrates how its curvaceous form relates to the immediate environment.

The house is named for Gilbert Segel and his wife Joann, who commissioned John Lautner to design a home for them in the 1970s. The project was a prestigious one—today, Carbon Beach is dubbed Billionaire's Beach—and the architect was an inspired choice. Having mentored under Frank Lloyd Wright, Lautner was known for his own brand of organic modernism and was much sought after by the L.A. cognoscenti.

American midcentury-modern style had its roots in Europe, drawing on works by the Bauhaus group and the International Style. While embracing the tenets of modernism and the application of cutting-edge technology and materials, the style also championed integration with nature and the creation of organic forms. Seen from the beach, the house appears to emerge from the sand—an elegant sweep of concave glass rising from nothing at its western end, through a single-story living space, to a two-story structure at its eastern end. You can see how

the line of the roof follows the contours of the mountain range in the distance—who would know that the busy Pacific Coast Highway rumbled between the two. The house is just part of the landscape.

The building's beach-facing façade is almost fully glazed. The concave line of the living room brings the outside in, while the convex line of the two-story structure pushes its rooms—the kitchen, bedroom, and study—out over the beach. This blurring of lines between nature and man is emphasized by the planting of bamboo, giant palms, and creepers both inside and out. Lautner's use of materials is also key: bold concrete structures and swatches of slatted wood interplay with each other to create a series of curved forms. While meeting the structural needs of the design—allowing the architect to create vast open-plan spaces—these materials are also decorative. On the one hand, it is thanks to their properties that they can achieve such beautiful shapes. But there is also warmth and color in the grains of the wood and the polished concrete surfaces. (SOU)

fig. b   fig. c (opposite page)

64

The concave line of the living room brings the outside in, while the convex line of the two-story structure pushes its rooms out over the beach.

fig. e

fig. d & e: Raw concrete is used for focal structural features, such as the staircase, fireplaces, and the kitchen island.

fig. f: Houseplants are pivotal in making a seamless link between the home's interior and what lies outside.

fig. f

Walstrom House

Clinging to a craggy rock face in L.A.'s Santa Monica Mountains, John Lautner's ultramodern Walstrom House could not be more at home.

Architect: John Lautner
Location: Los Angeles, CA, USA
Completion date: 1969

Walstrom House—named for its original owners—is like a huge tree house that has been built into the side of a step hill. The unconventional shape of the house is determined by the lay of the land, and yet the building looks so comfortable here, as if it tumbled down to this spot from the mountaintop like a boulder come loose in a storm. The architect, John Lautner, worked for some time with Frank Lloyd Wright and his design for Walstrom House reflects Wright's influence. Wright himself described his buildings as organic, and he strove to design structures that were at one with their natural surroundings.

What is impressive about this organic approach is that it makes no compromise with modernity. As Lautner demonstrates, a structure does not have to mimic the environment in which it sits in order to blend in. In fact, quite the opposite can be true. Take the Walstrom House: the exterior is predominantly wood, yet its application is far from rustic. Raised on a sturdy timber frame, the house is all clean straight lines, perfect proportions, and severe geometric shapes. Yet it is difficult to imagine a construction that better exemplifies being at one with nature. Echoes of natural forms can be seen in the deliberate asymmetry of the structure and the way in which the house seems to zigzag its way down the mountainside, following the path of least resistance. Inside, the house is no less modern, with its large-scale, open-plan rooms. Enter the building on its split level, follow the open staircase wherever it leads, and you will instantly be rewarded with unspoiled views into the woods beyond. Floor-to-ceiling glass has the effect of bringing the woods right into the home. And then there is the wood itself. Everywhere you look Lautner has used timber: to create the sculptural open staircase; to give texture and depth to the ceiling; to integrate functional elements, such as the bookcases in the living room; or merely to emphasize the beauty of the material itself, with its warm colors and fine figuring.   (SOU)

fig. a   fig. b (opposite page)

fig. a: A view of the house from above, wedged in between rocks and rampant forest.

fig. b: Stairs in the large, open-plan living room rise to a second level with views right into the treetops.

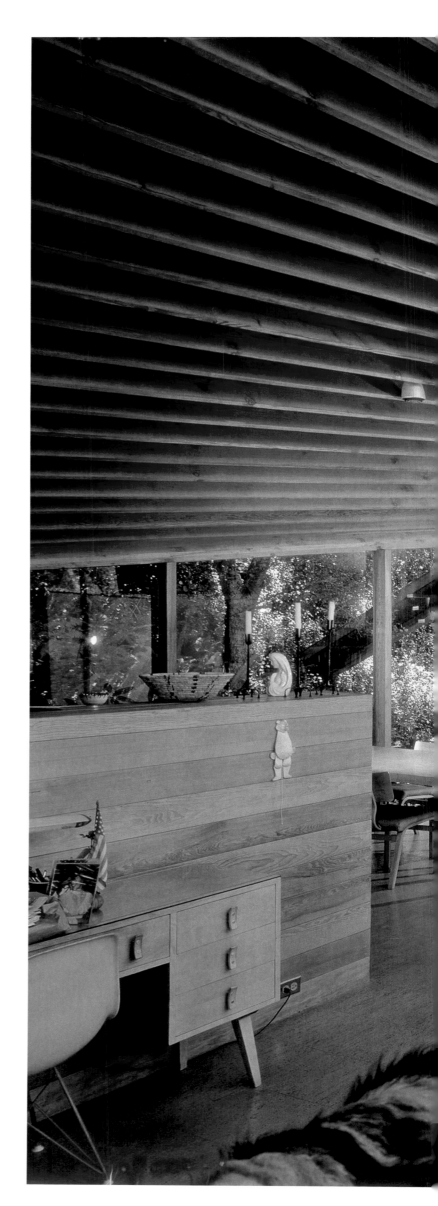

Schneidman House

Architect: A. Quincy Jones
Location: Los Angeles, CA, USA
Completion date: 1948

The interiors of this gem, created as an experiment in co-operative living near Los Angeles, revolutionized how public and private space was considered.

It might appear that the egalitarian principles of European modernism were diluted when crossing the Atlantic to encounter the individualistic culture of 1940s and 1950s California. This would be a simplification. The Mutual Housing Association, which commissioned the Schneidman House, was initially founded by a small group of studio musicians. They hired a design team headed by architect A. Quincy Jones, who devised between dissimilar functions, Jones blurred the previously highly ordered patterns of domestic behavior. A multi-purpose room, bright and open, became the center of the house, while the dining room and kitchen opened up to one another. The designer obliterated the traditional separation between the public act of food consumption and its preparation. The interior also reveals the novel nature of the house's structure. Jones was interested in creating a system of construction that could be shared across the development, yet adapted easily. The exposed post-and-beam ceiling is an important statement about the building techniques that this house shares with the others. However, recognizing the individual character of the family who owned it, the house boasts a great number of bespoke design features that relate to its wood paneling. Built-in furniture and cabinetry ameliorate and soften the rigidity of the house's structural system. The house hunkers into the landscape, sheathed for a large part in redwood, but also concrete and glass walls. Crowning its hilltop setting, the irregularly planned building expertly balances the social values of the Association with the individual demands of the owner. (ABR)

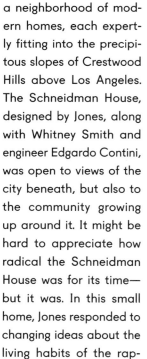

fig. a

fig. a: The approach to the house was conceived as much as a place of relaxation as a means of gaining entry.

fig. b: Kitchen and living space are not formally separated. The architect uses bespoke fittings as a partition.

fig. c: External concrete terracing was landscaped on top of the steep grade to create continuity with interior.

fig. d: The open-living dining space was designed to permit the largest possible appreciation of the views.

a neighborhood of modern homes, each expertly fitting into the precipitous slopes of Crestwood Hills above Los Angeles. The Schneidman House, designed by Jones, along with Whitney Smith and engineer Edgardo Contini, was open to views of the city beneath, but also to the community growing up around it. It might be hard to appreciate how radical the Schneidman House was for its time—but it was. In this small home, Jones responded to changing ideas about the living habits of the rapidly growing Californian middle classes. Eliminating traditional partitioning

fig. b

fig. c

fig. d

Smith House

Architect: Arthur Erickson
Location: Vancouver, Canada
Completion date: 1964

The second house that Arthur Erickson designed for modernist painter Gordon Smith is a classic: a key site in the making of a nation's artistic identity.

The artist Gordon Smith is one of the great pioneers of Canadian modernist painting, and his home, designed by the late Arthur Erickson, is one of the great examples of Canadian West Coast Modernist architecture. It is the second home that Erickson designed for Smith and his wife Marion. Although

fig. a

Whilst nearly all the vertical planes in the building are glazed, Smith's studio, which anchors one corner of the courtyard, is closed off and lined with plaster rather than wood, with natural lighting coming from above. The living room lies effectively across a small ravine in the solid granite that the house sits on. The bridge is elevated, providing an even greater appreciation of the view ot the water. Both in the living space and in the bedroom, walls are glazed and the house is rendered utterly open to the landscape, with the rough timber posts and cross beams providing a sense of security and warmth. This creates what is often grandly called a "promenade architecturale," a term which suggests that a visitor can simply circulate around the building enjoying diverse views and rooms: across the bridge, through the dining room and on to the terrace. It is perhaps unlikely they would do this. However, the landscaping is utterly continuous with the interior, and a series of outdoor rooms and terraces extend the house's living area into the surrounding forest. The house is sited amidst granite outcrops from when distant views of the sea can be glimpsed.   (ABR)

fig. a: Erickson wanted to make a house that retained the quality of the original site: a clearing in the woods.

fig. b & c: The internal plan and the exterior terraces have been conceived as a continuous promenade architecturale.

fig. d: Native wood has been used as both a weighty structural component and for delicately made fixtures.

clearly a modernist structure, the home built in 1964 strikes a strong contrast to the delicate steel constructions created in California in the decade previously. It is constructed from massive Douglas fir beams supported by similarly weighty posts in the same material and sits on a promontory above the Straits of Georgia in West Vancouver. Although bulkier than a Japanese house the lattice of post-beam members clearly betray Erickson's fascination with the architecture of that country. In addition, the house is built around a central courtyard which effectively recreates the original forest clearing, but in architectural form.

fig. b

fig. c

La Ricarda

Architect: Antoni Bonet i Castellana
Location: Catalonia, Spain
Completion date: 1963

This masterpiece of twentieth-century rationalist architecture demonstrates how structure, form, and materials alone can define the spaces within which we live.

fig. a

fig. a & b: La Ricarda sits within a pine forest minutes from the Catalan coast. The undulating roofs of the building emulate the soft treetops of the pines.

fig. c & d: At the center of the house, a vast open-plan living space combines kitchen, living room, dining area, and entrance hall under the arches of four roofs.

Set among pine trees close to the northeastern coast of Spain, Casa Gomis is better known as La Ricarda—a name the house shares with the estate on which it is built. The work of architect Antonio Bonet i Castellana, the house was commissioned as a private residence for clients Ricardo Gomis and his wife Inés Bertrand Mata in the 1950s. A single-story structure beneath a series of Catalan vaults, the building was hugely experimental for its time. The standout feature of this house is, most certainly, its gently undulating vaulted roofline. Low and wide, it mirrors the cloud-like treetops of the pines that surround it. Taking the porch as standard, the arches are raised on pillars, allowing for vast open spaces within—the depth of the arch, though shallow, is enough to give an impressive height to the interior. The floor plan is asymmetrical and dictated by use of space. Beyond the entrance porch, four arched units create a huge, central, open-plan communal space. The scale here is impressive: you only need to count the number of sofas and lounge chairs to see how generous this area is. Beyond it, and connected to it via glass-walled corridors, are the more private spaces—the bedrooms and bathrooms. Here and there one might stumble across an external terrace or courtyard—even a pond. True to rationalist theory, the building relies on the materials used in its construction—reinforced concrete and steel, glazed stoneware, and glass—to bring an aesthetic value to the work. There is great emphasis on proportion and geometric form. The building's façade is almost fully glazed, the arches filled with a ceramic lattice pierced with disks of colored glass. Inside, the rooms are whitewashed and bear little in the way of ornamentation, allowing the forms and materials to speak for themselves. Colors within the rooms are typically Spanish—warm yellows, browns, olive greens, and touches of pink, orange, and red. Shades have faded a little over the years, but are no less harmonious than they must have been more than half a century ago. (SOU)

fig. b   fig. c (opposite page)   fig. d (following double page)

fig. e: Within the large open room at the center of the house, the architect introduced decorative screens and wall dividers to create more intimate spaces.

fig. f & g: The house remains in the Gomis family and retains much of its period furnishings, including the Butterfly chair designed by Bonet, among others.

fig. h: Decorative devices such as this glass and ceramic wall were built into the structure of the building.

fig. i: Much of the house was glazed. In some areas, wooden slatted screens allowed inhabitants to regulate the amount of light coming into the room.

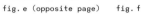

fig. g

The standout feature of this house is, most certainly, its gently undulating vaulted roofline. Low and wide, it mirrors the cloud-like treetops of the pines that surround it.

A Maestro with Italian Midcentury Flair

GIO PONTI

* November 18, 1891, Milan, Italy
† September 16, 1979 (aged 87), Milan, Italy

A select few are written down in history as pioneers of modern Italian design and architecture. Gio Ponti is the father of Italian modernist design, a tastemaker who co-created a phenomenon in Italian style and beauty.

Architect, designer, producer, publisher, writer, and thinker Gio Ponti was born in 1891 in Milan, the city that later became his playground for design and architectural adventures. He served in the military during

the First World War, from 1916 to 1918. After the war he studied at Politecnico di Milano, graduating in architecture in 1921. He began his career in partnership with Mino Fiocchi and Emilio Lancia from 1923 through 1927, Lancia then becoming his sole partner until 1933. In those years, Ponti became an important representative of modern classicism, what was known in Italy as the Novecento Italiano movement. ▷

COFFEE TABLE

Ponti designed the D.555.1 table for his house in Milan in the mid-50s. Beneath the glass tabletop, a hand-painted metal grid creates a simple but eye-catching geometric pattern.

83

He was very attracted to and inspired by Italian historical heritage and classic styles, which played a definitive role throughout his career. From the beginning, Ponti understood the design process as a complex idea, not limited to only architecture. He soon began to produce his own furniture pieces, as well as porcelain, ceramic, and maiolica objects for Richard Ginori, a well-established company that Ponti collaborated with enthusiasm for many years. His neo-classical designs for vases and other vessels created between 1923 and 1930 echo traditional Roman silhouettes, and highlight Ponti's refined skills in drawing and decoration.

LOUNGE CHAIR

In the D.153.1, designed in 1953, Ponti offers a long, gently reclining seat for maximum relaxation and comfort. There is a lightness to the tubular brass frame.

Ponti founded *Domus* magazine in 1928, a showcase of contemporary Italian design.

In 1928, Ponti founded *Domus* magazine, a groundbreaking publication that went on to be one of the most influential on architecture and design of the last century. Gianni Mazzocchi, a 23-year-old publisher who had moved to Milan from the Marche region, purchased *Domus* in 1929 and founded *Editoriale Domus*, which still publishes the magazine today. Many important designers and architects have served as editors at *Domus*, including Giuseppe Pagano, Melchiorre Bega, Ernesto Nathan Rogers, Cesare Casati, Andrea Branzi, and Mario Bellini. ▷

VILLA PLANCHART

Location: Caracas, Venezuela
Completion date: 1957

Villa Planchart is an expression of all of Ponti's incredible talents—from the structure of the building itself, to the furnishings within, and the classic 50s color palette with its muted primary colors. A change in ceiling heights adds dynamism, while built-in furniture brings cohesion and harmony.

In 1960, Ponti designed the Parco dei Principi Hotel in Sorrento, Italy, in which he furnished rooms with striking ceramic tiles with bold blue and white geometric patterns.

During the 1930s, Ponti moved forward with the new modernist style. He designed functionalist Casa Laporte on Via Brin in Milan, and in 1931 he founded Fontana Arte, an important producer of glass furniture and lighting. Among the most famous decorative pieces he created for the company is the geometric Bilia lamp, designed in 1931.

In the mid-1930s, Ponti received a huge architectural commission to design Palazzo Montecatini on Milan's Via della Moscova. Built together with engineers Antonio Fornaroli and Eugenio Soncini in 1936, the structure was one of the first rationalist buildings in Milan. The architect designed the complex modern office building with an attention to every single detail—from lighting, sinks, and door handles to clocks and bent steel-tube office chairs. This was the first project of Ponti's that highlighted his acumen in overall design solutions.

The postwar optimism brought a new colorful, flamboyant flavor to Ponti's work. In 1952, he partnered with architect Alberto Rosselli and engineer Antonio Fornaroli and entered the most prolific period of his career in both design and architecture. In 1950, he won the commission to design the 32-story Pirelli Tower in collaboration with

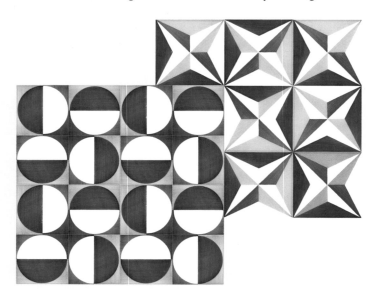

 HOTEL PARCO DEI PRINCIPI

> "The more minimal the shape,
> the more expressive it becomes."
> *Gio Ponti*

Pier Luigi Nervi and Arturo Danusso; construction began in 1956. This was the second skyscraper built in Milan and likely the pinnacle of Ponti's entire career.

As the Pirelli Tower attracted more attention, domestic and international commissions flooded into Ponti's office. He designed many buildings in Italy, Venezuela, Iran, Hong Kong, Netherlands, and the U.S. His architecture of the 1950s and 1960s achieved a perfect symbiosis of construction and decoration. Diamond-shaped structures were covered with refined relief decorative tiles to create works of art in all senses. He built a series of beautiful churches, including San Francesco in 1963, the church at Ospedale San Carlo in 1967, and the Taranto Cathedral in 1971; designed two Parco dei Principi hotels, one in Rome in 1956, and one in Sorrento in 1962; and created several housing and office buildings.

SUPERLEGGERA CHAIR

The "superlight" chair was Ponti's take on local vernacular furniture. He took the rustic form and gave it a modern twist. The back legs rise to form the upright supports for the backrest.

Probably the most striking of his projects during this time are three villas he built in Caracas and Tehran. Villa Planchart, Villa Arreaza, and Villa Nemazee are masterpieces in the joy of living. The most complex of the three was Villa Planchart in Caracas, commissioned by art collectors Anala and Armando Planchart in 1954. The house, dedicated to art, is a fascinating mosaic of bright colors and fluid shapes, showing Ponti's optimistic Italian style at its best.

During the 1950s and 1960s, the architect shined as a prolific furniture, product, and industrial designer. He created several icons of Italian modernist designs, including pieces for Cassina like the celebrated 1954 Distex arm-

chair and the 1955 Super-leggera chair. He also continued to design lighting for the Arredoluce brand, decorative tiles for Joo Ceramics and Ceramica D'agostino, silverware for Sabattini, and amazing sculptural enamel pieces for Paolo de Poli. He continued to build and design until his death in 1979.   (STE)

PIRELLI TOWER

Ponti's Pirelli Tower literally cut the corners off the traditional block-like skyscraper, giving it a more streamlined look. At the time of construction, it was the tallest building in Italy.

Clemmensen House

Light, bright, and colorful, this early—somewhat experimental—example of live-work architecture exudes 1950s optimism.

Architect: Karen and Ebbe Clemmensen
Location: Gentofte, Denmark
Completion date: 1953

In the years immediately following the Second World War, the Danish government offered loans to families who wished to build houses no larger than 130 square meters. Part of the government's far-sighted agenda was to encourage entrepreneurship and at-home offices. Houses could be extended to include areas for certain business uses, such as artistic practices. This combination prompted a number of Danish architects to create bespoke houses with adjacent drawing offices, none more impressive than that built by Karen and Ebbe Clemmensen. The house's design is experimental, providing huge insight into the couple's thinking and the later direction of their practice. Although they followed emerging trends out of the U.S., Karen and Ebbe Clemmensen were students of Japanese architecture. The house is interrupted by a number of light screens. In addition, the juxtaposition of tra-

fig. a   fig. b (opposite page)

fig. a: The chimney is a dominant feature of the building—a modern interpretation of a traditionally rustic form.

fig. b: Simplicity is key in this development; much of the furniture, such as this bench seating, is integral to the design.

ditional materials such as wood with simple modern ones is testimony to the Japanese influence. Built from lightweight aggregate concrete, the building is a simple, long, and low construction with a vernacular pitched roof and wooden frame. The chimney breast is an important intervention, conveying the true spirt of Danish *hygge* as opposed to a badly translated cliché of the term. Long and slender, the house reaches out into the landscape on a single story. The architects articulate the journey into nature with a warm, wooden-clad ceiling. The floor is more literally warm, as the house pioneers the use of underfloor heating—though the floors of the main hallway, the hall to the bedrooms, and the bedrooms themselves were originally covered with linoleum. The use of colors on the bespoke cabinets is extremely refined, dominated by pastel shades. In the entrance, a number of storage spaces are composed in a Mondrian pattern, which is picked up throughout the house. In the kitchen, cabinet doors have been created in a unique mid-century-modern color scheme of yellow, gray, and turquoise. Trims of turquoise have been added to the window sills. (ABR)

The house's design is experimental, providing huge insight into the couple's thinking and the later direction of their practice—both were students of Japanese architecture.

fig. c

KAREN AND EBBE CLEMMENSEN   CLEMMENSEN HOUSE

fig. d

fig. c & d: The prolif-
ic use of cedarwood—
for the frame of the
building and its pan-
eled ceilings—grounds
the building in its
natural surroundings.

fig. e: Ultramodern for
its time, the fitted
kitchen combines the
functional aspects of
the room with decora-
tive pastel paneling.

fig. e

Villa Sayer

Architect: Marcel Breuer
Location: Deauville, France
Completion date: 1974

Originally designed for the Alpine slopes, Villa Sayer in Normandy is the finest of residential works from Marcel Breuer. Striking structural engineering and refined interior decoration create a total work of art.

fig. a

fig. a: The dining room of the villa is furnished with Eero Saarinen's Tulip chairs, among others.

fig. b: The butterfly roof of the house creates a strong artistic statement, as seen from a distance.

fig. c & e: The living room of the house is dominated by a central diamond-shaped fireplace surrounded by an informal furniture ensemble.

During the 1960s and 1970s, Hungarian-born architect and designer Marcel Breuer, who was based in the U.S. at the time, built several projects in Europe. Concentrated in France, these included a brutalist ski resort, Flaine, in the French Alps. Construction began in 1960, and the resort became a landmark of modernist leisure architecture. More than 10 years later, Breuer received another exciting commission in France, this time from the Parisian Sayer family. After failing to commission Oscar Niemeyer to design their house, they became interested in Breuer, who was still in the middle of constructing the Flaine resort.

Breuer and his partner Robert F. Gatje first conceived the design of this house in 1959 for the English actor-director Peter Ustinov, who wanted to build a statement residence in Vevey, Switzerland. Unfortunately, it never happened. But when the architect showed the original plans to the Sayer family, they immediately fell in love and decided to build it on their site in Normandy.

Inaugurated in 1974 to the satisfaction and pride of all, Villa Sayer was lauded in the press by enthusiastic critics.

The structure of the house is composed of a hyperbolic roof that sits on three huge, diamond-shaped pillars. The butterfly-like roof structure completely covers the living space with floor-to-ceiling windows. Inside, the precise detailing meets the monumentality of the brutalist style. The interior includes canvas-covered walls, doors with metal abstract reliefs, and a huge sculptural fireplace in the middle of the living room. (STE)

fig. b   fig. c (opposite page)

fig. d

The interior includes canvas-covered walls, doors
with metal abstract reliefs, and a huge sculptural fireplace
in the middle of the living room.

fig. d, f, & g: The interiors feature custom-made decorative elements such as brutalist-inspired abstract doors.

INTERIOR DECORATION

RIDING THE FLAMBOYANT WAVE OF ECLECTICISM

— *Dawnridge* by Tony Duquette,
pp. 112–119

Fornasetti House

Architect: Piero & Barnaba Fornasetti
Location: Milan, Italy
Completion date: Ongoing

Walking through the rooms of the Fornasetti-house is like taking a whirlwind tour of this incredible artist's mind.

fig. a

fig. a, b, & f: Barnaba Fornasetti's home has everything: from sunburst mirrors on the walls, the classical seating in the library, to the red velvet handrail on the stairs.

fig. c & d: The bedroom with its cloudy wallpaper. Against the wall stands a cabinet with an architectural facade—a collaboration with Gio Ponti.

fig. f & g: Different rooms, same set-up. The sense of humor can be seen in the mirror-like arrangements of these two rooms.

Piero Fornasetti was one of the twentieth-century's most prolific designers. In a career that spanned more than 40 years, he produced as many as 13,000 different objects—the vast majority of which were paintings, homewares and scarves embellished with his characteristic black-and-white transfers. Among his favorite motifs were sunbursts and the face of the opera singer Lina Cavalieri. The soprano's visage featured in more than 350 different guises on plates alone, let alone glasses, trays, ashtrays, lamp bases, boxes or small tables, and paperweights. Fornasetti was influenced by the classical architecture of ancient Greece and ancient Rome, and by the works of Italian artist Giovanni Battista Piranesi—in particular, his neoclassical etchings, of which Fornasetti's décors are often reminiscent. Neoclassicism also provides a starting point for a tour of this intriguing home, a Milan townhouse, whose rooms have handsome proportions, large windows, and herringbone parquet flooring. And it is against this backdrop that the artist's mind reveals itself. First, there is color. Each room of the house

has walls painted in a strong classical color: a dark leafy green for the living room; crimson for a boudoir-style guest bedroom; mustard yellow for a work space; pale blue for the library; and a warm cream for the kitchen. Then, set against these flat colors, are countless examples of the artist's creations. The kitchen has a black-and-white newspaper-print floor, while butterfly transfers flutter upon every surface. In one of the bedrooms the walls are thick with Fornasetti's dreamlike clouds. Everywhere you look, there are plates, trays, cushions, and linens adorned with sunbursts, geometry instruments, coins, foliage, and, of course Cavalieri's face—whatever the designer had in his mind when he put pen to paper. Stepping into the library reveals the creative hub of the house and a most incredible collection of books and records. It is here that you can really start to understand what made the artist tick. After all, a mind with such prolific output must also have a rich input. (SOU)

fig. b   fig. c (opposite page)

PIERO & BARNABA FORNASETTI   <u>FORNASETTI HOUSE</u>

"This place is a house, a workshop, an archive, and a museum." *Barnaba Fornasetti*

fig. h: The kitchen table and chairs repeat the newsprint floor motifs and are embellished with Fornasetti's skittish butterflies. Above hangs a replica of a Murano glass chandelier.

Undisputed King of the Whiplash Curve

VLADIMIR KAGAN

* August 29, 1927, Worms, Germany
† April 7, 2016 (aged 88), Palm Beach, FL, USA

In designer Vladimir Kagan's work the American dream came true. A true tastemaker of modern American furniture design, the Russian/German immigrant became one of the most celebrated furniture designers of the second half of the last century.

Kagan was born in Worms, Germany, in 1927. His father Illi was a Russian cabinetmaker who learned

his trade in a First World War prison camp. The family lived a prosperous middle-class Jewish life in an apartment above his father's workshop. In 1938, when Vladimir was just 10 years old, his family escaped Germany and arrived in New Jersey.

Illi Kagan adapted to American life very quickly. He opened a

"His furniture became an icon of modernity, an essential reference."
The New York Times

furniture repair shop and soon his own cabinetmaking shop in New York. His customers included extravagant designer James Mont, decorator to New York's gangsters. The young Kagan helped his father in the workshop and showed a natural talent for drawing in school. Kagan's early focus was on painting and sculpture, but in the following years he

became eagerly attracted to architecture and design. He graduated from the School of Industrial Art in 1946 and went on to study architecture at Columbia University. His style at the end of the 1940s, and later his furniture designs, grew out of his many inspirations and experiences—the modernist designs of his native land, where Bauhaus was having its moment, the antique furniture of his father's shop, cabinetmaking, and a deep interest in fine arts. ▷

KAGAN APARTMENT

Kagan's designs were not limited to stand-alone forms. He also designed modular seating as displayed in his own eclectic apartment in New York.

"My greatest satisfaction is when the sketch looks as though I had drawn it from the final piece."
Vladimir Kagan

Designed in 1950, Kagan's Serpentine sofas epitomizes the mid-century aesthetic for sculptural, organic forms. Typical of his style, are the sofa's asymmetrical shape and low back.

At the end of the 1940s, Kagan still worked for his father, supplying furniture for department stores or custom interiors. But he soon realized that he was much more interested in designing the pieces than executing them as his father did. Unlike his young contemporaries, designers George Nelson or Charles Eames, who devoted their work to mass production, Kagan became fascinated by every detail of a piece. Each of his designs became an original and an expression of an artistic idea.

In 1948, Vladimir Kagan opened a shop on East 65th Street. From the beginning, he created a multidisciplinary space, selling not only his own furniture creations, but also ceramics, textiles, and art. The shop attracted many avant-garde artists and became the place to be. Soon, Kagan met Hugo Dreyfuss, retired Swiss lace manufacturer,

ceramic artist, and textile designer. He invested in Kagan's business, and in 1950 Kagan-Dreyfuss was born. The partnership lasted ten years and spanned the golden age of Kagan's productivity.

During this period, the design developed his signature style of organic free-form shapes. In addition to managing his own business, he spent time developing furniture designs and custom-made interiors. Among his most famous designs of the period were upholstered furniture pieces like the elegant Serpentine sofa, with its oversized kidney shape. ▷

Kagan was a true master of the dynamic form. Standing at 187 centimeters tall, his aluminum Stalagmite lamp (see also in his apartment on the left) was his answer to the standard lamps with a shade.

In the 1960s, Kagan closed his shop and ended his partnership with Dreyfuss. At the time, he experimented with new materials and added new clients to his roster. Monsanto Chemicals commissioned him to design Room for Total Living in 1963 at the Park Avenue Armory exhibition. This project opened the door to new ventures for Kagan. He designed the futurist interior of Monsanto's House of the Future at Disneyland in Anaheim and the stereophonic installation for General Electric Company at the 1967 World's Fair in Montreal. These projects were designed in the trendy space-age aesthetic, but unsatisfied with only corporate collaborations, so Kagan continued with individual designs as well.

The 1970s signaled a new direction for Kagan's style. He left behind his organic shapes, which would end up in baroque and mannerist styles, and devoted himself to developing a new type of seating. The Omnibus sofa was an extremely successful product, a modular concept that could be adapted to almost any use to create the ultimate interior landscape.

Kagan liked to play around with the idea of transparency. Many of his designs involve pieces in which the structural element is almost invisible, as in this sofa and stool.

Kagan also mastered tables of all different types. His tri-symmetric bases made of glass or marble and his colorful mosaic tops are inspired by roots and tree-node formations. They celebrate material and artistic expression and as Kagan has said: "art and beauty are part of everyday living." In his Unicorn series, inspired by Constantin Brancusi's Bird in Flight sculpture, Kagan used aluminum to cast the organic bases for chairs and sofas.

Other successful designs from the era include his Floating sofa, Contour armchair, and Capricorn outdoor furniture collection. These products also attracted artist, socialite, and celebrity clients. Among them were Gary Cooper, Lily Pons, Xavier Cugat, Marilyn Monroe, and the Rosenberg family, a famous clan of gallerists.

Each of Kagan's designs became an original and an expression of an artistic idea.

Kagan closed his factory in 1987 and founded his new studio, the Vladimir Kagan Design Group. At the end of the 1990s, his furniture returned to the limelight. As creative director of Gucci, fashion designer Tom Ford ordered 360 Omnibus sofas to furnish every Gucci store worldwide. And Kagan himself started a brand-new adventure in his seventies, selling his creations under the Vladimir Kagan Classics brand. He also became a darling of the collectors and the auction houses, his original pieces selling for tens of thousands of euros. He passed away in 2016, still working until his very last days and presenting brand new pieces in his last show at New York's Carpenters Workshop Gallery.   (STE)

Having crafted such fine shapes from wood during the 1950s, Kagan turned his attention to Plexiglass at the end of the 1960s, exploiting both its strength and its sculptural properties.

Dawnridge

Architect: Tony Duquette
Location: Los Angeles, CA, USA
Completion date: 1949

Sunset Boulevard meets the Doge's Palace in the theatrical interior of this extravagant Beverly Hills home.

fig. a

fig. a: An ornate gondola sits in the still water outside an Indian temple on the grounds of Dawnridge.

fig. b, f, & g: Rooms with ceilingfrescos and heights of over five meters are decorated with the most lavish furnishings from far and wide.

fig. c, d, & e: The living room is more akin to a Venetian salon than a Beverly Hills lounge, with ornate chandeliers, pierced fretwork, and faux malachite paneling.

Dawnridge was one of several private residences owned by Tony Duquette, the designer and jewelry maker who wowed Hollywood with his incredible talent for over three decades. From the 1930s to the 1960s and beyond, he worked on several interior design projects, many in collaboration with his artist wife Elizabeth Johnstone. Dawnridge is considered one of his greatest works. Today, the exquisite rooms remain a showcase of Duquette's extraordinarily flamboyant style thanks to his former business partner Hutton Wilkinson, who now lives in the house with his wife Ruth. It is hardly surprising to discover that Duquette designed sets and costumes for Hollywood movies and plays—such is the theater within the walls at Dawnridge. There is barely a surface that has not been decorated in some way—and then some! Duquette had a great sense of whimsy and tremendous flair. In styling this house, he was hugely influenced by the Venetian gothic style of the fifteenth and sixteenth centuries, evident in the slatted ceiling and fretwork pelmet in the living room, and the black-and-white checkered flooring. Much of the furniture in the house has a Duquette twist on rococo style—a Louis-XV-style bergère armchair with leopard-print upholstery, for example. But Duquette also had a fine collection of antique pieces that included an ornate seventeenth-century Piedmontese

secretary desk and an elegant eighteenth-century Venetian console. Ornaments throughout the house betray a more oriental taste—from Balinese Buddha figures and ceramic elephants to pagoda-style pot stands, ornaments, and birdcages. Duquette used a host of clever theater-set techniques to fake the look of luxury materials. The malachite paneling in the living room is really just the brushwork of a skilled artist. Screens in the drawing room contain a series of sunbursts, at the center of which are chrome hubcaps. It is an approach that Hutton Wilkinson has continued; he spray-painted the original silk curtains in the drawing room to achieve the look of taffeta.   (SOU)

fig. b   fig. c (opposite page)   fig. d (following double page)

Duquette was hugely influenced by the Venetian gothic style of the fifteenth and sixteenth centuries, evident in the slatted ceiling and fretwork pelmet in the living room, and the black-and-white checkered flooring.

Streamlined Surrealism and the Human Form

CARLO MOLLINO

* May 6, 1905, Torino, Italy
† August 27, 1973 (aged 68), Torino, Italy

Carlo Mollino was a renaissance man whose oeuvre embraced the cultural and technological world of his time thanks to his unadulterated love of life and innovation. The prominent Italian architect and designer was born in Turin in 1905. His early childhood drawings of

cars, airplanes, and houses show evident signs of his later interests. He was also influenced by a close friendship with his father Eugenio, who worked as an engineer and immensely supported his son's interests. After graduating with an architectural degree from the Polytechnic University of Turin in 1931, Mollino collaborated with his father, and, before long, his first architectural assignments presented themselves. ▷

CASA DEL SOLE

Mollino designed a series of beds for the Casa del Sole in Cirvinia, Italy, in 1953. They were fashioned simply from oak slats, but with jewel-like brass and formica elements.

"Everything is permissible as long as it is fantastic."
Carlo Mollino

apartment, designed for his own personal use, was the first in a series that illustrate Mollino's style, which crystallized into an organic yet bizarre, eclectic modernism. In Casa Miller, rococo mirrors, classicistic clocks, and an ancient horse head sculpture are complemented with his own ingenious designs; his sliding ceiling light, a mirror shaped as ancient Venus, and, primarily, the airy system of suspended draperies create a dreamy space. Mollino used the apartment as a lavish set for his photographic interests.

In the following two assignments—the Devalle I and II apartments from 1939 and 1940—the architect

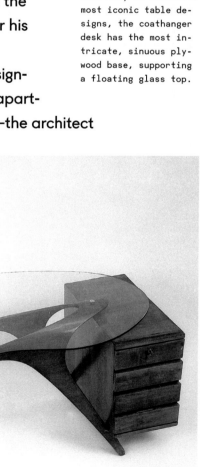

PLYWOOD COATHANGER DESK

Like many of Mollino's most iconic table designs, the coathanger desk has the most intricate, sinuous plywood base, supporting a floating glass top.

His work in the fields of interiors and architecture began in the late 1930s and spanned the 1940s into the 1950s. While Mollino continued pursuing his design career, he also discovered a passion for sports. His friends introduced him to car racing, skiing, and acrobatic flying. He also taught architecture at the Polytechnic University of Turin from 1952 to 1970. During the last years of his life, he devoted most of his time to his last passion: photography.

But interior design was the essential medium for Mollino's creativity. Be it in the organic interiors of private residences or in a distinctive approach to furniture design, his work delivers maximum impact. His first interior design venture began in 1936 with Casa Miller. This private

played a surprising game with the interior, which verges on rococo and psychedelia. Mirrors, excessively decorated upholstered furniture, and a bedroom covered with pink satin serve as evidence of his supreme interior surrealism. His pioneering eclectic approach hints at postmodernism, well before this movement was actually named. With the following Minola (1944–1946), Rivetti (1949), and Orengo (1949) apartments and their morphology, Mollino showcases aesthetics that ultimately inform his designs throughout the 1950s.

TEATRO REGIO

Location: Turin, Italy
Completion date: 1973

Carlo Mollino was commissioned to refurbish the Regio Theater, decades after the building had been devasted by fire. The womb-like auditorium, emphasized by the prolific use of red and the curvaceous lines of the box seating is illuminated by a luxurious cascading chandelier by Gino Sarfatti. The red theme continues into the foyer, again iluminated with elegant chandeliers.

The furniture pieces, exclusively designed for the individual apartments, represent the acme of Mollino's design production. The organic shapes of wood, produced in formal experiments by the Apelli and Varesio workshop in Turin, highlight the unusual sculptural quality of his work. In the 1950s, the designer worked on several other assignments: furniture for the Musa exhibition at the Brooklyn Museum in New York, the interior for the Casa Editrice Lattes publishing house (1951–1952), and the RAI auditorium. He also furnished the design of the ▷

Mollino always styled his own shoots, choosing clothes to match the visually impressive environments of his own designs.

Casa del Sole chalet in Cervinia with furniture pieces inspired by traditional Alpine culture.

One of Mollino's last interior designs includes Casa Mollino—another private apartment for his creative endeavors—which he gradually worked on until 1968. He never actually lived in the apartment, its rooms designed according to rich symbolism and mythology. Today, the apartment is owned by Fulvio Ferrari, an Italian curator and collector who wrote several books on Mollino with his son Napoleone. He opened the apartment to the public to give testimony to Mollino's legacy. Ferraris brought his work to light for a contemporary audience, giving collectors and artists a fresh source of inspiration. Every year, many famous artists such as Patti Smith, Robert Wilson, and Jürgen Teller visit Casa Mollino to see the masterful creativity of the unorthodox architect and designer.

Mollino was obsessed with the female figure, and the smooth curves of his furniture designs were often informed by the female form. He made many portraits of women during his career.

Mollino's architectural career began in 1934, when he finished the headquarters of the Farmers' Association building in Cuneo in collaboration with V. Baudi di Selve. The following project, the Turin Equestrian Association headquarters, built from 1937 to 1940, demonstrates his style in a very convincing way. The large complex, which includes a riding hall, stables, and rooms for social events, represents an original interpretation of an organic style. Purely white surfaces, combined with sharp geometrical facing and wavy moldings, link period modernism with the Baroque architecture of Turinese master Guarino Guarini. The spectacular stairwell with glass railings crowns Mollino's exquisite style.

In 1947, the architect finished an impressive design of a sledge-lift station, as well as the Lago Nero guesthouse, which connects a ▷

modernist ground floor and a large terrace on conical pillars with a top section made from wood. The gabled roof is inspired by traditional Alpine architecture. Mollino blended local architectural tradition with the most

progressive construction trends of the time. Be it the expressive design of the Furggen funicular station, the redesign of the traditional Garelli Alpine chalet, the design for the suspension of the Truss House, or the constructed Casa del Sole chalet and hotel in Cervinia, he always interconnected the postwar organic concept with mountain rusticity. A commissioned family house by Lake Maggiore, built from 1951 to 1953, was also conceived in a very expressive way. The house is pushed above the ground by concrete beams and equipped with a typical gable roof.

The most challenging assignments awaited Mollino toward the close of his life. The Turin Chamber of Commerce was built from 1964 to 1972 in collaboration with ▷

CASA MOLLINO

Location: Turin, Italy
Completion date: 1968

Lavishly decorated in his own idiosyncratic style, Mollino's house in Turin was full of color, ornament, and exquisite textiles. Much of the furniture was of his own design, although other iconic pieces made an appearance—Le Corbusier's chaise longue and Saarinen's Tulip chairs. The home also housed Mollino's collection of female portraits.

"Only when a work is not explainable other than in terms of itself can we say that we are in the presence of art." Carlo Mollino

Carlo Graffi, A. Galardi, and A. Migliassi. The brutalist and futuristic expression of the building, which bears a geometrical grid of rounded windows, lacks characteristics featured by Mollino in his works from the 1950s. To the contrary, the monumental extension of the Teatro Regio in Turin, finished in 1973, gives a more typical impression.

The brick organic mass of the Teatro Regio and its large glazed surfaces refer back to the radical architecture of Guarino Guarini once again. The interior of the lobby, with a geometric crystalline ceiling and brick reliefs, contrasts with the fluid space of the auditorium. Collaborating with Carlo Graffi and Adolfo and Marco Zavelani Rossi, Mollino achieved an unusual dynamic composition. The auditorium, constructed in the shape of an egg, is topped with spectacular lighting by Gino Sarfatti.

In addition to architecture and design, Mollino was fascinated by technology and speed, and actively contributed to motor racing, skiing, and acrobatic flying. Together with Enrico Nardi and Mario Damonte, he designed the Bisiluro 750 sports car, made in Nardi's car-body workshop. This extraordinary futurist vehicle took part in the 1955 Le Mans competition. Unfortunately, it never finished the race and after three hours ended up outside the racing track. Acrobatic

flying was an even bigger passion for the architect's adventurous mind. He took part in many well-known competitions and became one of the best Italian pilots in this discipline. He also designed several aircrafts. However, none of them were realized.

Mollino was also a downhill skier, a skill he developed after meeting Austrian downhill skiing champion Leo Gasperl in Livrio in the

1930s. Gasperl was invited to Italy to train the Italian national downhill skiing team. The pair shared a passion for style and speed, and struck up a friendship, paying attention to every single detail in the hierarchy of skiing—from the perfect jump to overly precise bindings and elegant outfits. Books such as *Downhill Skiing* by Leo Gasperl from 1939 and *Introduction* ▷

The high-back lounge chair that Mollino designed for a house in Turin in 1946 is, like many of his designs, luxuriant, sensual, and anthropomorphic.

to Downhill Skiing by Carlo Mollino codify their technical and visually impressive discipline within the sport.

Last, but not least, photography was Mollino's indispensable medium, into which he channeled his desires, interests, and modern visions from the start of his career. Not only did the designer and architect take photos of his interior designs and architectural implementations, he also focused on shots of flying, skiing, and women—many of whom served as significant muses. Most impressive among his many photo series, artistically speaking, are the nudes, which he started to shoot in the second half of the 1950s. Mollino took photos of his models from the lens of both an artistic and a fashion photographer. The carefully selected settings, usually in his own apartment or Villa Zaira, another space he bought and renovated in

the early 1960s, became dreamy backdrops for his models. He always styled his own shoots, choosing clothes to match the visually impressive environments of his own designs. The results represent delicate and sensual nudes that reflect the artist's prolific catalog and hedonistic nature. He took photos and later color Polaroids of nudes in complete secrecy for more than 20 years.

Turinese architect, designer, photographer, pilot, race car driver, and skier are titles upheld to the highest standard by Carlo Mollino, one of the most fascinating creative minds of the last century. Design and architecture were given completely new dimensions through his endless creative passion and love for life. Mollino was a designer all his own.   (STE)

CASE DEVALLE

Location: Turin, Italy
Completion date: 1940

Influenced by the surrealist works of artists like Salvador Dali, Mollino designed an apartment for the architect Giorgio Devalle, in which the lavish furnishings were coated in sumptuous velvets, furs, and silks. Features included padded walls and ceilings, and a lip-shaped couch in the style of Dali's Mae West sofa.

Jaretti House

Architect: Sergio Jaretti
Location: Turin, Italy
Completion date: 1966

One of the last witnesses of the heroic times of Italian midcentury modernism conceals his secrets inside this fantastic villa in the middle of a lush garden.

fig. a

fig. a & c: The multi-level living space is a dynamic architectural composition made of bricks, its decorative qualities highlighted by the design of the staircase.

fig. b: Before Jaretti died, he added a vault structure on the roof of the house, with the plan to create another floor.

Until his recent death at the age of 88 in 2017, Sergio Jaretti was still working and recalling the golden years of Italian design culture. The architect, like his colleague Elio Luzi, was a student of Carlo Mollino at the Polytechnic University of Turin. After graduation, they co-founded Luzi Jaretti studio and unveiled the magic of free architectural expression. This is most strikingly expressed in one of their first projects, Casa Obelisco, an apartment building near the city center. They designed a highly eclectic townhouse overflowing with organic shapes and expressive decorative elements. The result was an unprecedented symbiosis of organic modernism and art nouveau inspiration.

During the 1960s, they dramatically changed their style and started to build more abstract and refined houses made of bricks. In the mid-1960s, Jaretti built his own house at the foot of Monte Aman in Turin with the help of Luzi. The house is a refined sculptural composition made of perforated bricks, a signature of both architects at the time. Within its walls lies an eclectic and decorative world that favors the architect and his

work. Clean rectangular brick walls provide a space for Jaretti's inventiveness, where many different styles and multicultural influences converge. Afghan carpets hang and lie almost everywhere, antique furniture stands alongside his own modernist creations, and art deco cabinets from his parents' home create a fantastical eclectic mix.　(STE)

fig. b　fig. c (opposite page)

Jaretti designed a highly eclectic townhouse overflowing with organic shapes and expressive decorative elements. It was an unprecedented symbiosis of organic modernism and art nouveau inspiration.

fig. d

SERGIO JARETTI

JARETTI HOUSE

fig. d: Today's library
used to be a rounded
concrete greenhouse full
of vegetation, lit by a
glass skylight.

fig. e & f: The interior
style of the house is
very eclectic, mixing
many different histor-
ical pieces, such as
art deco cabinets and
radical Italian-designed
lighting and rugs.

fig. g: Jaretti designed
this custom-made dining
table especially for the
house. He complement-
ed it with art nouveau
chairs.

fig. h: The bathroom
features blue and white
vegetation-inspired
decoration across the
walls and ceiling.

fig. f

The house is a refined sculptural composition made
of perforated bricks, a signature of Jaretti and Luzi's many
apartments around Turin.

SERGIO JARETTI   JARETTI HOUSE

The Living World Sculpted in Bronze

LES LALANNE

François-Xavier Lalanne: * August 28, 1927, Agen, France; † Dezember 7, 2008, Ury, France
Claude Lalanne: * Unknown , 1924, Paris, France

During the 1960s and 1970s, fine art mingled very closely with decorative art. Using interior objects and design as autonomous forms of artistic expression, avant-garde decorators of the time may very well have been fine artists first and foremost. Interiors became artistic interventions, where furniture doubled as sculptural pieces and

lamps as luminous, kinetic objects. Among the artists who crossed into the decorative arts environment are François-Xavier and Claude Lalanne. Just as other French artists, including Yonel Lebovici or Jacques Duval-Brasseur, they primarily based their work on animalistic ▷

Les Lalanne sculpted many animals, fruits, and vegetables. On occasion, as here, a work might also have an anthropomorphic element, such as this bronze apple's human facial features.

François-Xavier gave his animalistic forms a practical function, most often using bronze to shape them into furniture pieces: a bar in the form of a hippopotamus; a rocking chair as a metal bird; a monumental bed as a dodo bird; a fireplace as a baboon; a chair as a frog; and a table consisting of a huge statue of a locust. Insects or reptiles were occasionally worked into the designs as well—animals certainly not high up on the adoration list. In these pieces, the contrast elicited a recoiling and an appreciation of the beautiful at the same time. One of François-Xavier Lalanne's favorite animals was the rhinoceros, which he portrayed in

Many of the Les Lalanne sculptures also formed a function of some kind: here a chimpanzee supports a tabletop; on the previous page, a sheep provides a stool for the rhinoceros desk.

forms. A glamorous 1970s elitist interior might have been met with surrealism, becoming a bestiary of design. A husband-and-wife duo, the couple is known for their monumental sculptures in the shapes of various animals.

François-Xavier was born in Agen, France, and studied sculpture, drawing, and painting at Académie Julian, while Claude Lalanne was born in Paris and studied architecture at the École des Beaux-Arts and the École des Arts Décoratifs. François-Xavier met Claude Lalanne at his first gallery show in 1952. At the time, the couple moved in artistic circles more than in those of decorators and designers, associating with Max Ernst, Man Ray, Marcel Duchamp, and Jean Tinguely.

In 1964, they exhibited together for the first time. From then on, they were regarded as a single entity by the public: Les Lalanne. But the artistic duo rarely collaborated on their pieces, instead co-creating their own objects, even if in very similar styles. Nature was a strong inspiration, François-Xavier sculpting animal themes, Claude favoring vegetation—the results straddling the line between fine and decorative arts.

LES LALANNE

life-size, functional sculptures using a range of materials. In 1971, he created Blue Rhinoceros together with Japanese designer Kazuhide Takahama for the Italian experimental company Simon. Made from enamel metal, the piece could be opened up to become a desk or a bar. Les Lalanne were hugely inspired by surrealism and its dreamy, anxious juxtapositions. Salvador Dalí often used animal forms in his speculative objects, such as the lobster telephone he created in 1936 for English poet Edward James.

During the 1960s and 1970s, Les Lalanne rose in popularity and interest

"The supreme art is the art of living."
Francois-Xavier Lalanne

among the public and art critics alike. In the mid-1960s they produced one of their most famous designs: realistic bronze and wool sheep sculptures, which were often presented in a herd. These could be seen in the interior of the glamorous Milan apartment designed in 1969 by Gae Aulenti for Italian philanthropists and collectors Giovanni and Marella Agnelli.

Other important clients of Francois-Xavier and Claude Lalanne included Pierre Bergé and Yves-Saint Laurent. While Francois-Xavier designed several pieces for their apartment, including the exceptional custom-made bar, Claude Lalanne's gilt ▷

Modern man meets medieval maidens: much in the spirit of the art world during the late 1960s and early 1970s, Les Lalanne installations were as surreal as their creations.

metal castings from the body of supermodel Veruschka were incorporated into Saint Laurent's 1969 Empreintes collection. The custom-made bar sold at Christie's in 2009 for 2,753,000 euro. The couple also became known to the larger French public when singer Serge Gainsbourg selected a work by Les Lalanne, the man with the head of a cabbage, for the title and cover of his 1976 album. The bestiary of the French decorators has been brought back into view in recent years. Represented by prestigious New York–based Paul Kasmin Gallery, their work has become

This pair of brass chaises was designed by Claude Lalanne in 1980. The design is much less ornate than the majority of her work, much of which has sculptural floral and vegetal motifs.

"They are not furniture, they are not sculpture—call them 'Lalannes'."
Claude Lalanne

part of several important collections and can be seen in public spaces around the world. The animal motif has influenced several contemporary designers. Julia Lohmann established herself in 2005 by creating a leather bench in the shape of a cow torso, and Hella Jongerius created a frog table from solid walnut wood for Galerie Kreo in Paris. The dynamic couple that is Les Lalanne has stood the test of time, enduring in the spirit of these pieces the world over.　（STE）

Perhaps their most realistic sculptures, Les Lalanne sheep were sculpted in bronze and finished with real fleeces. Gathered together as a herd, they were incredibly convincing.

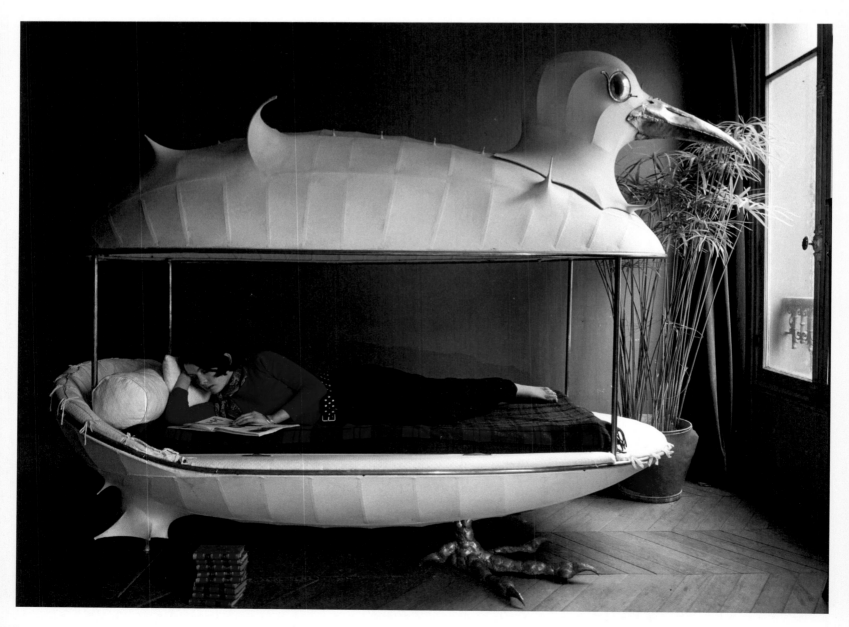

TURNING THE LIVING SPACE INTO AN EXPERIMENTAL ENVIRONMENT

— *Palais Bulles* by Antti Lovag,
pp. 220–225

La Renardiere

Architect: Étienne Fromanger
Location: Jouars-Pontchartrain, France
Completion date: 1975

What better way to furnish this iconic 1970s home than with seminal designs of the same era—all cartoon-like forms and clashing colors.

fig. a

fig. a, c, & d: The vaulted arch, the dominant structural form of the building, is repeated in decorative details throughout.

fig. b: Chairs by Verner Panton surround an Eero Saarinen table; in the background sits Gaetano Pesce's Series Up 2000 chair and ottoman.

fig. e: Rich, midnight blue walls and floor engulf the bed to create a calm sleeping environment.

fig. f: Poppy pinks and oranges vie with each other for attention in a laid-back lounge area.

Although often grouped together with the maisons bulles type, this house designed by Étienne Fromanger, brother of the painter Gérard Fromanger, exists in a class of its own: a bioclimatic house which sits half-submerged in the ground and covered in greenery as a means of using the environment. The house has been given a brilliant 1970s makeover which manages to both match and elevate the original rustic concrete vaulting. Admittedly, the original owes as much in architectural style to the vaulted cellars as to the sci-fi bubble houses. But the way in which its new owner Olivier Aucler has added furniture pieces such as Frank Gehry's cardboard Wiggle chair (made in 1972) and the Serie Up 2000 chair and ottoman designed by Gaetano Pesce in 1969, match and reinterpret the generous arches and curved roof forms.

Unlike other maison bulles, the house sits directly on the ground and is covered with foliage. This has the advantage that the thermal insulation is superb. The temperature rarely drops below 11 degrees centigrade and never exceeds 23 degrees, which is a perfect range. The pay-off for this extremely comfortable

ambient temperature is the general lack of natural lighting deep within the house. It creates an environment which is like a protective cocoon, but this puts a priority on using vibrant colors in internal spaces and making the most of the dramatic floor-to-ceiling glazing in the living room and master bedroom.

The house may not provide huge opportunities for hanging art on the wall but this has prompted the owner into even greater levels of ingenuity, building up wooden banquettes for seating which also act as risers on which framed artworks can sit. Indeed the whole project is a labor of love. Olivier Aucler first saw the house as a teenager. Having enjoyed a successful career, he bought the house when it was put up for sale. The fifty-year-old fan of beautiful objects and 70s design then proceeded to give the 350-square-meter space his own personal touch. "I saw a permanent dream. Every day on my way home, I think I'm lucky," says Aucler, who would sell the house for nothing in the world. (ABR)

fig. b   fig. c (opposite page)

fig. d (previous double page)   fig. e   fig. f (opposite page)

This house exists in a class of its own: a bioclimatic
house which sits half submerged in the ground and covered
in greenery as a means of using the environment.

Denmark's Designer from out of Space

VERNER PANTON

* February 13, 1926, Gamtofte, Denmark
† September 5, 1998 (aged 72), Copenhagen, Denmark

jumped into the colorful and organic lines of consumerist culture and hippie psychedelia. Among the most successful designers of this period is Danish designer Verner Panton.

Panton revolutionized Danish design and embodies the era and the modern designer in general. During his career, he created futuristic designs in vibrant and exotic colors using a variety of materials, especially plastics. Panton then broke with the tradition of Danish cabinetmaking, becoming famous for his new space-age pop designs.

After graduating with an architectural degree from the Royal Danish Academy of Fine Arts, Copenhagen, in 1951, he worked at the architectural practice of Arne Jacobsen, the legendary Danish architect and furniture designer. After two years, he started his own design and architectural office. He became well known for his innovative proposals, including

Panton's pendant lamp design was a very simple design—literally one hemisphere suspended within another. Available in bright colors, it became an icon of 1960s popular culture.

During the 1960s, new pop-culture influences were making their way into interior design. Elegant modernism was steered into new directions by the swinging 1960s and its artistic movements, particularly American and British pop-art and the optimistic age of space exploration. New forms of interior design abandoned the elegant curves of the 1950s and

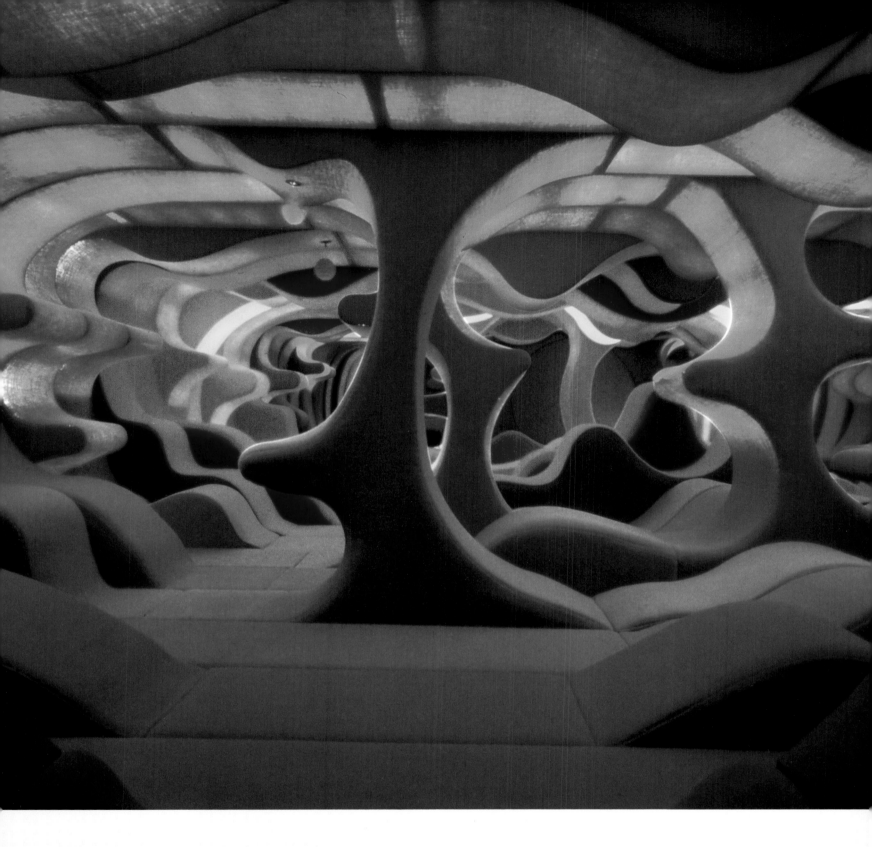

"The main purpose of my work is to provoke people into using their imagination." *Verner Panton*

a collapsible house (1955), the Cardboard House, and the Plastic House (1960). These projects exhibit Panton's endless interest in new materials, innovative solutions, nomadic structures, and experiments of any kind.

The early part of his career was dedicated to the development of unconventional seating designs, adapting forms, materials, and structures. His Cone chair (1958), Heart chair (1959), and Peacock chair, created one year later, were all manufactured by Danish brand Plus Linje. Bright colors and striking shapes reigned. The soft upholstery that drove his designs for these interior sculptures informed Panton's later organic landscapes.

His most famous design, the Panton chair, is produced today by Swiss company Vitra. One of the most well-known chairs   ▷

VISIONA 2

Panton's Fantasy interior for Bayer at the 1970 Cologne Furniture Fair looks no less futuristic now than it did almost half a century ago, so avant-garde was the designer with his concepts.

153

PANTON CHAIR

Panton's S-shaped chair was revolutionary for its time. Never before had it been possible to produce a cheap, stacking chair in bold colors and from one single piece of molded plastic.

of the last century, it was the first single unit cantilevered chair made of molded plastic. Panton had been working on its design since the 1950s, making a series of sketches and design drawings before creating his first model. In the mid-1960s,

Vitra's former chairman Willi Fehlbaum decided to work with Panton on developing this remarkable design. It was a leap, an abandonment of the traditional form of a chair. Panton produced a cold-pressed model using polyester strengthened with fiberglass. In 1968, Vitra initiated serial production of the final version, which was then sold by the Herman Miller furniture company. An icon of 1960s design and furniture design was born. Today, the chair is one of Vitra's bestsellers. It is produced in polypropylene and available in many bright colors, and also in a children's version.

"One sits more comfortably on a color that one likes."
Verner Panton

Panton's seating designs of the 1960s were individual predecessors of his total furnished environments. His radical and psychedelic interiors were completed by curved furniture, wall upholstering, textiles, and lighting. With these compact interior landscapes of vibrant colors and soft organic shapes, Panton created a new way to experience the interior environment, free-spirited and without conventional pieces of furniture.

He also designed pieces that encouraged users to interact with furniture in new, playful ways. His Living Tower is an unorthodox interior object with no similarities to traditional pieces. First released in 1969 by Herman Miller, Vitra has been producing it since 1999. This organic upholstered sculpture has four seating levels to sit and relax on and engage with in many ways, as if in a treehouse.

Among his most famous environments is one he created for German chemical corporation Bayer in 1970 at Cologne's Furniture Fair. Bayer organized a series of installations called Visiona from 1968 to ▷

A joint stand in 1972, that Panton decorated for the furniture and lighting manufacturers Fritz Hansen and Louis Poulsen. The highlights were the new Pantonova wire chairs.

Despite their futuristic looks, Panton's interiors were not without form or formality. Colors were selected to complement one another and there was symmetry in the arrangement of furniture.

1971, commissioning the leaders of new pop and space-age designs including Joe Colombo, Olivier Mourgue, and Verner Panton. Each year, one of the designers created their own vision of a futuristic interior landscape onboard a boat on the river Rhine. The aim was to promote various synthetic products in connection with home furnishings. Panton was commissioned no less than twice to design this installation. Visiona 2 in 1970 showed a colorful upholstered landscape with various seating and relaxation options in a psychedelic aesthetic. In terms of design history, this installation is regarded as one of the major spatial designs of the second half of the twentieth century.

It is in this spirit and with his own furniture and lighting designs that Panton created a complete interior for the new premises of Spiegel publishing house in Hamburg in 1969. Panton designed the entrance area with courtyard and lobby, the canteen and the bar

areas, the swimming pool for the employees in the basement of the building, the rooms for the editorial conferences and the lounges, and even the color schemes for the hallways of the administration and editorial high-rise buildings. While most of the spaces have since been redesigned or damaged, the canteen survived as a great example of a 1960s interior-design vision.

During the 1970s and 1980s, Panton continued to work on his projects in interiors, furniture, lighting, and textiles, as well as in accessories, toys, and artistic objects. The designer died in 1998, but not before receiving the Queen of Denmark knight's cross of the Order of Dannebrog.   (STE)

"A failed experiment can be more important than a trivial design."
Verner Panton

Torres Blancas

Architect: Francisco Javier Sáenz de Oiza
Location: Madrid, Spain
Completion date: 1969

A monument of the modern Madrid skyline, Torres Blancas stands among the most expressive brutalist high-rises in Europe. Its architecture reveals an important chapter in Spanish modern architecture.

fig. a

fig. a: The apartments of Torres Blancas feature curved walls and multi-level spaces in an organic style.

fig. b: With its rounded balconies, the tower is a masterpiece of organic sculptural architecture and unique in European architecture of the time.

Modernist tower Torre Blancas is an impressive twentieth-century monument in the Spanish capital of Madrid. Built between 1964 and 1969, the 71-meter-tall structure is the finest work of celebrated Spanish modernist architect Francisco Javier Sáenz de Oiza. With it he created an icon of international brutalist and Spanish organicism architecture. Before studying architecture in Madrid, Sáenz de Oiza went to school in Seville, a historically rich city with an extraordinary heritage of Arabian architecture. The elaborate decorative and organic structures of Seville's old Moorish buildings echo in his later projects. After studying abroad in the U.S. in 1949, he became a professor at the School of Architecture in Madrid and began working on independent projects. The monumental brutalist structure of Torre Blancas represents a high point in Sáenz de Oiza's career. The high-rise apartment building was designed as a rhythmical series of interconnecting cylindrical volumes crowned by round overhanging balconies. Celebrated for its original form, it also stands as one of the most complicated and innovative reinforced concrete structures of the era. Absent are the typical rectilinear forms associated with concrete apartment complexes built throughout Europe in the 1960s.

The building was commissioned by enlightened developer Juan Huarte, who wanted to build two similar towers next to each other. In the end, just one tower was realized by Sáenz de Oiza and his collaborators, young architects Juan Daniel Fullaondo and Rafael Moneo. Moneo went on to become one of the most celebrated Spanish architects and win the prestigious Pritzker Prize.

Curvilinear design and the rounded shapes of the brutalist façade became signatures of this tower, whose interior echoes its organic exterior. In the foyers as well as the apartments, elliptical windows and huge cylindrical decorative forms shape the interior of this massive concrete structure, crowned by a top-floor roof terrace with pool and garden.   (STE)

fig. b   fig. c (opposite page)

fig. c: The terrace on the top is an outdoor extension of indoor living. This leisurely zone includes a curvy pool as well.

fig. d: The entrance area's ceiling features monumental rounded forms, echoing the exterior of the structure.

fig. e: The interior of one of the apartments is furnished with Joe Colombo's Elda armchairs, which have formal similarities to the architecture.

fig. f, g, h, & i: A newly furnished apartment is equipped with historical icons and new designs to create a contemporary take on modernism.

Curvilinear design and the rounded shapes of the brutalist façade become signatures of this tower, whose interior echoes its organic exterior.

Built between 1964 and 1969, this 71-meter-tall
structure is the finest work of celebrated Spanish
modernist architect Francisco Javier Sáenz de Oiza.

fig. g

fig. h

fig. i

Kunstoffhaus FG 2000

Architect: Wolfgang Feierbach
Location: Altenstadt, Germany
Completion date: 1969

Little-known German designer and engineer Wolfgang Feierbach envisioned a house as an industrially produced machine. In a small village in the middle of Germany, he succeeded in realizing his dream.

fig. a

fig. a: Wolfgang Feierbach's own house, built in a small German village, is made of prefabricated plastic modules.

fig. b & c: Feierbach realized two FG 2000 houses. The first one became his office after he successfully started his plastic business.

fig. d: Everything in the first completed house was custom-made in plastic, including this striking staircase leading from the entrance area to the former living area upstairs.

Designer, inventor, and engineer Wolfgang Feierbach dedicated his entire life to the development of plastics and their use in design and architecture. His brand FG Design was founded in the mid-1960s in the provincial town of Altenstadt, near Frankfurt am Main in Germany. At the same time, he began to produce plastic furniture in a contemporary organic pop-art style and developed a system for the construction of plastic prefabricated houses.

His dream to develop industrially manufactured homes ended with only two examples realized. The first of these, designed in 1969, has plastic modules forming the façade of the first level, which floats above the masonry-constructed ground floor. Today, the house is used as storage and office space for Feierbach's extensive archive. The glamorous interior, with its colorful textile pop-art ceiling, built-in plastic cabinets, and sculptural plastic stairs, was designed as a space for entertaining, where Feierbach hosted glamorous dinners and parties for his friends. After refurbishing the house just a few years after it was completed, it became the offices for Feierbach's venture into designing and producing plastic elements for architectural use. FG Design mastered the production of airport counters as well as

furniture highly inspired by the work of Dieter Rams. Though it never happened, Feierbach had at one time asked Rams to collaborate.

Feierbach designed a second, more complex home for his family during the 1970s. The interior surprises with its diverse and rich decorations. Feierbach's own furniture from the 1960s is combined with his later creations, most showcasing bold postmodern aesthetics, such as the spectacular architecture storage systems and library. The staircase, lit by a group of pop-art chandeliers, is covered with furry colorful textiles in motifs of abstracted moving figures. The main living room is divided into a lounge area with a large library and Leica projector on one side, and the kitchen and dining area on the other. The latter space is dominated by a central dining table, futurist lighting, and plastic sculptural-looking postmodern cabinets. Mixed with natural objects and sentimental artistic decor, the home is a living monument to the visionary, utopian ideas of Feierbach. (STE)

fig. b   fig. c (opposite page)

The interior surprises with its diverse and rich decorations. Feierbach's own furniture from the 1960s is combined with his later creations, most showcasing bold postmodern aesthetics.

fig. d

fig. e, f, g, & h: Details of plastic futuristic elements, including control panels and built-in storage systems, are prime examples of the forward-thinking designer's innovations.

fig. i: The figurative colorful graphic decorates the textile surface of the stairwell.

fig. j: Wolfgang Feierbach furnished the dining room with his own chairs and table.

fig. e

fig. f

fig. g

fig. h

fig. i (opposite page)   fig. j

Mixed with natural objects and sentimental
artistic decor, the home is a living monument to the
visionary, utopian ideas of Feierbach.

Windmill Home

Architect: Lou Jansen
Location: Turnhout, Belgium
Completion date: 1967

A home of two halves, Lou Jansen's windmill achieves a sensitive balance between the nineteenth-century original and the latest in contemporary design.

fig. a

fig. a, c, f, & g:
Jansen preserved just enough of the building's original features to maintain an element of rural, rustic charm.

fig. b, d, e, & h:
White, molded-plastic surfaces dominate the new elements within the windmill—no attempt is made to mimic the old in the new.

A verdant suburb of Antwerp, Turnhout is an unlikely destination for any dedicated fan of modernism. The area, though, is littered with a number of beautifully finished midcentury modernist houses. Because they were not photographed or publicized at the time of their construction, they remained largely unknown to the wider world. Thus, the work of Lou Jansen is little known beyond Belgium—but acclaim is greatly deserved. His simple steel-frame structures in glass and brick are invariably partially submerged while extending out from the foliage of the wooded suburbs. Woning Mil, which Jansen built for his brother in 1962, is a glass and brick pavilion that sits low amid birch and elm to great effect.

It is remarkable then that Jansen bought himself a nineteenth-century stone windmill to live in in 1967. Instead of a set piece of minimalism inveigling itself into the Flemish woodland, Jansen's house is a vertical agricultural building, which he converted first into a studio and then into a family home. Jansen chose the mill because he could never imagine a modernist home as groundbreaking as he would like it to be, whereas with the mill he did not need to claim authorship.

That is not to say it is without incredible ingenuity. Internally, Jansen used plastics and metal to clearly delineate the difference between the original structure, including

a good part of the actual milling machinery and riveted structural components, and the new elements he introduced. The kitchen is a plastic monocoque inserted into the stone structure: a cocoon with integrated fittings. The space that has been changed the least is on the ground floor: a room into which carts were driven so grain could be loaded or unloaded. The large vaulted brick space has been painted white and now serves as a dining room. (ABR)

fig. b   fig. c (opposite page)

fig. d

Jansen chose the mill because he could never imagine a
modernist home as groundbreaking as he would like it to be.

fig. e

fig. f

fig. g

fig. h

Lagerfeld Apartment

Architect: Memphis Milano
Location: Monaco
Completion date: ca. 1983

For a short time during the 1980s, fashion designer Karl Lagerfeld's penthouse in Monaco paid homage to postmodernism and, specifically, to Memphis Milano.

Founded in 1981, and spearheaded by architect and designer Ettore Sottsass, Italian design group Memphis Milano took an unprecedented departure from conventional design. At the group's core were a number of like-minded architects and designers who set out to challenge the modernism that had dominated much of the twentieth century. In doing so

considered him an "unparalleled interpreter of the mood of the moment." In his penthouse, Lagerfeld painted the walls in shades of dove and slate gray and installed matte black rubber flooring. Even the art on the walls was monochrome and featured huge nudes by Helmut Newton. There could be no better backdrop for his shrine to Memphis. Not only are all the iconic works here large-scale pieces by Sottsass, Michael Graves, and George Sowden—but there are also light fittings, ornaments, and TVs. The inclusion of architectural structures is a common theme, as in the upper section of Graves's dressing table in the bedroom. Plastic laminates with abstract or animal-print designs were also widely used, as in Sottsass's Beverly Cabinet in the living room. Pieces frequently combined luxury materials with inexpensive ones or looked to the past for their ornamentation and style. Above all, there was wit and humor—in the bold, unexpected use of color; in the seemingly impractical lack of symmetry; and in Sottsass's idea that, while a table might have four legs, not "all four legs have to look the same." (SOU)

fig. a

fig. a: Lagerfeld sits at a Pierre Table designed by George Sowden, with Riviera Chairs by Michele De Lucchi.

fig. b, c, d, & e: Seminal Memphis pieces include Michael Graves's Important Plaza Dressing Table; Ettore Sottsass's Beverly Cabinet, Peter Shire's Brazil Table, and Michele De Lucchi's Pacific Wardrobe.

fig. f: Masanori Umeda's Tawaraya party ring takes center stage in the living room. In the background, Sottsass's Aztec iconic Carlton Bookcase.

they turned the tenets of "good design" on their head, setting completely new boundaries, or, rather, no boundaries at all. For Memphis, the success of a piece no longer adhered to the form-follows-function mantra of modernism, but to its aesthetic appeal—its visual impact. The result was a diverse collection of bright and colorful furniture and homeware. Sometimes challenging, sometimes shocking, Memphis designs maximized on quirky juxtapositions, unusual materials, bold patterns, and witty gestures. Though short-lived, postmodernism was hugely influential, and it comes as no surprise that Lagerfeld took to it in a big way. After all, Vogue magazine

fig. b

fig. c

fig. d

fig. e   fig. f (following double page)

Casa Maui

Architect: Etorre Sottsass
Location: Maui, HI, USA
Completion date: 1994

A showcase of postmodernist style, Sottsass's design for Casa Maui in Hawaii is a riot of color, texture, and form—it is Memphis from top to bottom.

It is no surprise that the interior of this unique house by the Italian furniture designer Ettore Sottsass is stunning. Known for his key role within the Memphis collective of designers, Sottsass created a house full of humourist, historicist details: a staircase with a sculptural bannister, arched doorways and a series of work in wood, created the custom bed for the master bedroom. It is however very much Sottsass's vision: a gesamtkunstwerk for the Milanese designer who detailed all of the interiors, including the furnishings, such as vintage Hawaiian koa lounge chairs and Hyatt side tables of his own design in the living room. Throughout the house one finds works by Sottsass for different companies. In the office within the house stands a floor lamp for Treetops and a chair for Olivetti. The first model for the house that the designer created sits in pride of place in the studio along with many of the drawings. It is a work of art within a work of art, which sits on top of a hill on the Hawaiian island of Maui.

Rendered in colored stucco, the exterior is legible as a series of interlocking volumes in different hues. Green, yellow, and dark brown volumes intersect and are abutted by a cherry red tower with a pitched roof and a shiny steel garage. Sottsass was also responsible for the landscaping on the property, including a wooded area that shades the home from the street and a pond to the rear of the property in the shape of a Tylenol pill. (ABR)

fig. a

fig.a: The façade is project a collage of forms, yet the whole is carefully considered in terms of scale and proportion.

fig.b, c, d, & e: Bright colors, an eclectic choice of materials, and postmodern furnishings selected by Sotsass himself capture the witticism of the movement.

wall-mounted metal rungs in the master bathroom, which looks like a ladder but is in fact a series of towel rails. Much of the furniture is bespoke or inbuilt. Sottsass planned units to house a number of the client's collections, including vintage radios and a perfume collection. The house—designed for a jeweler who produced Memphis work—is something of a shrine to Memphis: it includes a number of Sottsass pieces, such as his Mini Totem earthenware sculptures; a painting by Nathalie Du Pasquier, one of the original Memphis designers; and a chair from by Michele De Lucchi, who cofounded Memphis. Renzo Brugola, who not only designed for Memphis but built much of the early

fig. b

fig. c

fig. d

fig. e

Brazilian Underdog and Master of Brutalism

EDUARDO LONGO

* June 26, 1942, Brazil

Brazilian architectural history is not just about big names like Oscar Niemeyer and Paulo Mendes da Rocha. Dozens of other lesser-known architects contributed to its legacy as well. One in this cast of characters is Eduardo Longo, master of brutalist and alternative organic

architecture. During the late 1950s, Brazilian architecture began to change. The elegant curves and light structures coming out of Rio de Janeiro lost their dominance in favor of newer brutalist and sculptural architecture from São Paulo. It was during this time that the young Eduardo

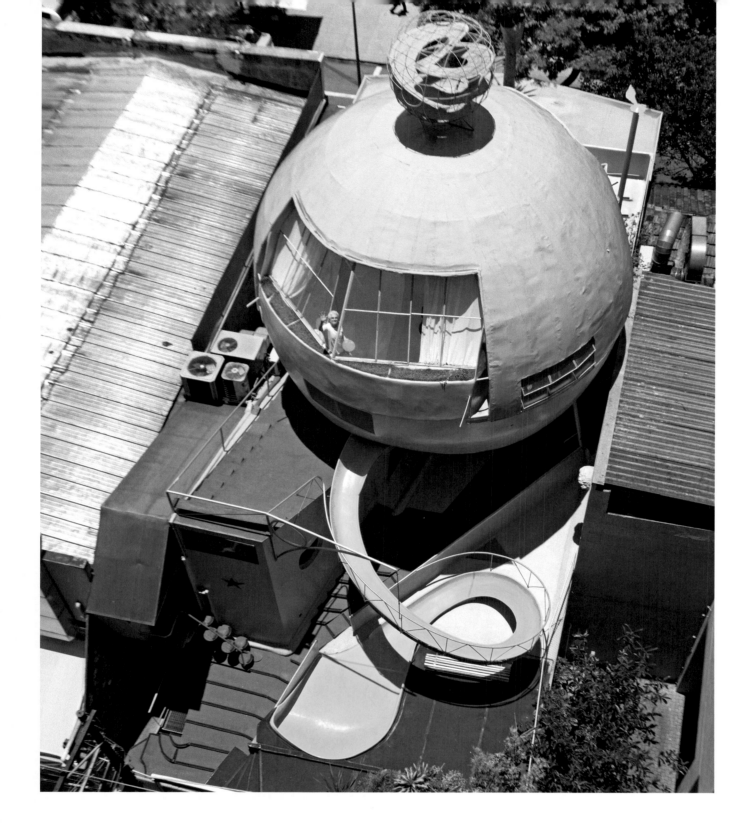

From 1964 to 1970, Longo designed and built several houses in the municipalities of São Paulo, Rio de Janeiro, and Guarujá.

Longo entered Brazil's architectural scene. Born in 1942, Longo graduated from FAU Mackenzie Presbyterian University in 1961, three years before the military dictatorship began. Thus he experienced many of the politically turbulent and culturally rich moments in the country's recent history. From his first project, he experimented with new creative discourses of architecture and was interested in deeper structural building strategies. He symbolically hid the interior of a house from outside, where the political regime of military revolution was taking hold. Architects like Rodrigo Levéfre, Marcos Acayaba, and others utilized new structural forms to hide dwellers in the home rather than open them to the landscape as the postwar modernists had. ▷

CASA BOLA

Location: São Paolo, Brazil
Completion date: 1979

Almost resembling an amusement park attraction these days, with its sky-blue exterior and gimmicky yellow chute, Casa Bola was more of a space-age marvel when built in 1979. This fantastic sphere literally looked as if it had landed overnight on the roof of a house in São Paolo.

concrete with local materials. Low masses of concrete roofs cover the shady living spaces, lit by refined skylight openings.

The most impressive of these houses is the 1968 Casa Guper, conceived as a coastal refuge for leisure. The owner wanted a space to listen to music, cultivate plants, and collect works of art, so Longo based the plan on overlapping functions within the environment and without conventional dormitories. In the second stage of the project, the architect added extra bedrooms and bathrooms. The house was designed for Milton Guper, ▷

Longo designed his first house in 1964. Casa do Mar Casado defined his work, which centered on artistic freedom, singular formal investigation, and the questioning of the architectural status quo. The one-story structure is constructed of irregularly composed flat concrete surfaces, a modern bunker that protects against both the hot climate and nervous political changes. Longo made use of raw concrete, as did his contemporaries and fellow representatives of São Paulo's Paulista school. But he went further, using it in a freer, more sculptural way as seen in his residential projects to come.

From 1964 to 1970, Longo designed and built several houses in the municipalities of São Paulo, Rio de Janeiro, and Guarujá. Pernambuco's beach developments were rapidly growing in the mid-1960s thanks to Brazil's economic miracle, becoming a playground for experimentation. Many important architects of the time built houses in the area, which became one of the most valued addresses in the whole country. Longo's beach houses are sensitive sculptural wonders, blending

<u>INSIDE CASA BOLA</u>

The rooms of Case Bola were just as space age as its spherical structure. Almost all of the surfaces where painted white and had smooth rounded edges.

Inside the houses, Longo created free-spirited open-space living with organically shaped built-in furniture.

an enlightened client who had commissioned famous Brazilian architect Rino Levi to design his 1951 São Paulo home. Longo himself was inspired by Levi's design and used rhythmical skylight openings to create an impressive outdoor/indoor space, lined by raw stone walls.

In the 1970s, Longo entered a critical process of reviewing his personal and professional values, marking a turning point in his career. After many projects under his belt, he was left unsatisfied and began to question his production. Instead of designing more houses, he took some time out to study the contemporary architecture and utopian visions of Richard Buckminster Fuller, Japanese Metabolists, Yona Friedman, and Archigram. He was very attracted to the newer utopian thinking and idealistic visions for the architecture of the time.

CASA GUPA

Location: Guarujá, Brazil
Completion date: 1967

The house that Eduardo Longo designed for Milton Gupa was one of harsh surfaces. The architect used reinforced concrete to create the shell, leaving it raw and exposed in the home's interior. Walls made of sheet glass, stone slab flooring, and huge rough-hewn stone columns completed the brutalist look.

Longo experimented with new creative discourses of architecture and was interested in deeper structural building strategies.

Location: Guarujá,
Brazil
Completion date: 1964

As with Longo's other
works, the façade of
the Casa do Mar Casado
in Guarujá gives noth-
ing of the building's
interior away. Step
inside, however, and
you discover a cathe-
dral-like space (for
fans of brutalism, at
least), in which the
gently raked concrete
roof climaxes in a
skylight through which
light floods the room
below.

Therefore, Longo moved into his countercultural phase. He became part of a new generation looking for freedom and who criticized the establishment and dictatorship. The counterculture movement manifested its concerns in cinema, music, theater, literature, journalism, and fine arts. Longo closed his office and abandoned conventional architecture to dedicate himself to the research of experimental ball-shaped structures. The aim was to construct spherical modular housing units that were industrially produced and then anchored in mega-structures. His utopian idea resulted in two Bola Houses (1972–1982). The architect began building one of them in the center of São Paulo in the mid-1970s. Made of circular metal tubes distributed in meridians, it was anchored to the original reinforced concrete

structure. The metal structure was then coated with canvas and covered with mortar, a solution based on the system of construction of boat hulls. Inside, the architect created free-spirited open-space living with organically shaped built-in furniture. During the construction of this experimental structure, Longo decided to finish his own residence, where he is still living out his utopian dream today. (STE)

Ford House

Architect: Bruce Goff
Location: Aurora, IL, USA
Completion date: 1949

Three circles form the perfect layout for Bruce Goff's Ford House in Illinois, one of the most fascinating modernist creations of the late 1940s.

fig. a

fig. a & d: The circular cozy interior of one of Bruce Goff's organic masterpieces is divided into different levels and features beautiful decorative elements.

fig. b & c: The Ford House was designed as a rich and spectacular composition of geometry and decoration, as were most of Goff's houses.

Ford House in Aurora, Illinois, is one of the most fascinating projects by Oklahoma-based architect Bruce Goff, who built hundreds of organic and stylistically varied houses across the U.S. during his extensive career.

Goff worked with an unbelievable imagination, designing houses according to his passion, state of mind, and a given site, which always defined the finished form of the building. The Ford House was designed in 1949 for celebrated artist Ruth Van Sickle Ford, director of the Chicago Academy of Fine Arts at the time. The spectacular home consists of three circular volumes: one central living space and two side bedroom wings. Goff worked with the circle as an ideal shape for living, creating a democratic and friendly environment for the open-minded client.

The structure was built of anthracite coal, steel, glass, cedar, and hemp to create an original mosaic of exotic materials and forms. The main living space is 15 meters in diameter, and the façade is divided in half. On one side is a massive wall constructed from coal and inserted pieces of raw glass; on the other side is the semi-interior space under a red steel cage-like structure. The roof of the house is made of shingles and follows the tradition of native folk architecture. Varied living zones and levels highlight the circular living space. The central

sitting area is situated around the sunken kitchen and dining area, with a stove in the middle. Above it, the huge lounge area is elevated on the central pillar. A beautiful dome-like structure with an expressive geometric ceiling of cedar wood is highlighted in the central roof's rounded skylight opening, with its rhythmical grid of red steel beams.

The house provided endless inspiration for artist Leo Saul Berk, who spent his childhood there. He became an artist thanks to the space, which he reflects on in many of his installations and sculptures. (STE)

fig. b   fig. c (opposite page)   fig. d (following double page)

Wharton Esherick Studio

Architect: Wharton Esherick
Location: Malvern, Australia
Completion date: 1966

The dean of American craftsmen: self-designed, hand-built Pennsylvania studio is a testament to the American Arts and Crafts pioneer's intuitive creativity.

The studio furniture movement is an important part of American twentieth-century design culture. Influenced by the early Arts and Crafts movement, the studio furniture makers worked more as autonomous sculptors and craftsman rather than modernist designers collaborating with companies and employing technological innovations. The American studio

his own handwork and furniture designs, which also took inspiration from Native-American culture. In 1926, he began building his own studio in Malvern, which became a long-term passionate project until 1966. There are five structures on the site of this large wooden retreat: Esherick's home and studio; the 1956 workshop, designed together with Louis Kahn; the 1928 German expressionist—inspired log garage, which now serves as the museum visitor center; his woodshed; and the recently reconstructed expressionist outhouse. The look of his home and studio represents an unorthodox mix of influences and forms, with everything designed to the very last detail and built by Esherick himself. Strong artistic expression is highlighted in the massive stone walls and organic wooden roofs outside. Inside, Esherick created a total work of art. His hard-edged furniture pieces sit around massive tree-trunk pillars and an organic twisted staircase—probably the most striking feature of the house. Today a dedicated U.S. National Historic Landmark, Esherick's hilltop studio/residence has been preserved much like it was when the artist lived and worked there. On exhibit are also more than 300 of his works. (STE)

fig. a

fig. a: The exterior of the studio looks like a set design from 1920s German expressionist films.

fig. b: All the details of the interior were finished according to the central concept of the structure by Esherick himself.

fig. c: Wharton Esherick created a total work of art in the interior, including his ladder and bookshelf. Some of his sculptures are also on display.

craft scene of the second half of the last century included famous artists such as Georges Nakashima, Paul Evans, Sam Maloof, J. B. Blunk, and Wendell Castle. But one of the most notable pioneers was Wharton Esherick, who was already active during the 1920s and 1930s in Malvern, Pennsylvania. Working in different types of wood, he created furniture highly inspired by the German expressionist movement of the time, taking from the dynamism and spirituality of forms of influential German architects such as Hans Poelzig and Erich Mendelsohn. Esherick implemented their sculptural style into

fig. b   fig. c (opposite page)

The strong artistic expression of Wharton Esherick's
studio is highlighted in the massive stone walls and
organic wooden roofs outside. Inside, the sculptor created
a total work of art.

fig. d: The rusticity of folk art meets avant-garde shapes and exquisite craftsmanship in Esherick's designs, including spectacular abstract flooring.

fig. e, f, & g: The kitchen features Esherick's designs in every single detail.

fig. h: Among the most important contributions to design from Wharton Esherick are his elaborate studio furniture pieces.

fig. i: The main sculptural staircase and built-in seating area were made from rough pieces of wood, a favorite material of the designer.

fig. f

fig. g

The studio furniture movement is one of the
strongest in the twentieth-century American applied arts
scene and Wharton Esherick a true pioneer.

Al Struckus House

Architect: Bruce Goff
Location: Woodland Hills, CA, USA
Completion date: 1982, resp. 1994

With the Al Struckus House, organic master Bruce Goff left a powerful testament. This private Californian residence and his last built project is a masterpiece of space and form.

fig. a

fig. a: The interior of the house is a complex and refined labyrinth of curvy spaces and forms, for which Bruce Goff is famous.

fig. b & d: The seating area in the kitchen is furnished with rare Goff-designed chairs and a Louis Poulsen Artichoke lamp hanging above the table.

fig. c: The exterior of the house consists of a sculptural cylinder with a series of four eye-like windows.

fig. e: The main living room is situated on the top floor of the house and composed of rhythmical openings.

Oklahoma-based wizard of American organic architecture Bruce Goff built only a few projects in California. One of them was also his last draft, whose design was, completed right before his death in 1982. Intended for retiring aeronautical engineer Al Struckus, the house in Woodland Hills, Los Angeles, is a tall cylindrical structure. From the outside, it is highlighted by futuristic-looking windows, resembling both alien creatures and the pure beauty of the natural world. One can enter the space through a huge wooden rotating door with a beautiful abstract stained-glass window at its center. Abstract images of stained glass were a signature of the architect.

For the next decade after Goff's death, his student, architect Bart Prince, oversaw the completion of the design in close collaboration with Struckus. The structure was not completed until 1994. As with all of Goff's designs, the Al Struckus House embodied a perfect symbiosis of general construction solutions and precise decorative details. The home has four floors; the ground floor contains only an entrance area and small storage, while the first and second floors offer a dramatic organic landscape. Curved floors and double-ceiling spaces resemble an artificial cave. The house—now owned by Kevin Marshall, head of preparation at the

J. Paul Getty Museum—culminates at the top floor with the seating and lounge area. While the circular windows on the staircase are dramatic, a series of smaller windows in a dynamic grid pattern create a beautiful mosaic of light and space. The house is one of only a few of Goff's built projects with a more vertical than horizontal character. Despite this, it is well constructed and has remained intact after its share of earthquakes. Looking at the floor plan makes clear why Bruce Goff is one of the masters of organic architecture. Shaped like a turtle, the plan showcases nature as the architect's biggest source of inspiration. (STE)

fig. b   fig. c (opposite page)

The house, Goff's only residential design in
California, is also one of his few built projects with a
more vertical than horizontal character.

Sleeper House

Architect: Charles Deaton
Location: Genesee Mountain, CO, USA
Completion date: 1963

Charles Deaton's sculptural house stands proudly above the mountains of Colorado as a strong statement of organic space-age architecture.

For fans of American modernist architecture, the cities of Boulder and Denver, Colorado, have much to offer in organic architectural heritage. Architect Charles Haertling adapted Frank Lloyd Wright's organic modernism to new forms during the 1950s and 1960s, building several houses in the area. Each project differed from one another, though all were surprising with spectacular and original forms.

he started designing mostly commercial buildings. He designed several bank buildings and sport complexes.

His own aerodynamic house, which was also his only residential design, sits on Genesee Mountain near Golden, Colorado. Deaton, who built it with the help of Clifford M. Delzell, ran out of money before the house was finished, so he never lived in it. The structure looks like a flying saucer floating above its remote forest landscape. The interior design of the house reflects the fascination with new forms of living during the period. An open-space living area becomes a compact interior landscape with built-in lounges and sitting areas.

Famed director Woody Allen chose the house as a backdrop for his 1973 sci-fi comic movie Sleeper, where the interior plays a main role. Software millionaire John Huggins purchased the house in 1999 for 1.3 million dollars. He built a large addition that had been designed by Deaton, with Nick Antonopoulos, before Deaton's death in 1996. He also commissioned Deaton's daughter, Charlee, to design the interior, which was completed in 2003. (STE)

fig. a

fig. a: The striking futurist form of Sleeper House sits atop the mountains and overlooks the impressive landscape.

fig. b: The organic staircase was designed according to the sensual aesthetic of the whole structure.

fig. c & d: Today, the curved interior is furnished by classics of international modernism such as Eero Saarinen's Womb Chair.

fig. e: The spacious bathroom features an abstract mosaic and asymmetrical windows in Deaton's signature aerodynamic style.

While his Willard House is a variation on the classic Wright aesthetic, his Brenton House is an unorthodox concrete white bubble-like structure, which highlights organic architecture in an almost futurist way.

The Sleeper House, built by architect and engineer Charles Deaton, followed Haertling's vision and gave it a new 1960s futurist, pop-art look. Deaton was trained in design and engineering during the Second World War at a Lockheed plant in California. After the war and with no formal education in architecture,

fig. b

fig. c

fig. d

fig. e

Casa Amalia Hernández

Architect: Agustín Hernández Navarro
Location: Mexico City, Mexico
Completion date: 1970

The heritage of ancient Mayan architecture comes alive in the work of brutalist master architect Agustín Hernández Navarro. His 1970s projects are strong modernist statements.

fig. a

fig. a & b: The exterior of Casa Amalia Hernández highlights strong sculptural elements of radical geometry, typical of Hernández Navarro's work.

fig. c: The interior is also based on the monumental appearance of geometry, as this rounded corridor shows.

Architect Agustín Hernández Navarro is one of the masters of the Mexican modernist movement, but his work has remained largely in the shadows of the more famous Luis Barragán or Ricardo Legorreta. Hernández Navarro's architecture stands apart, staying outside of most historical movements and categorical tendencies.

He started his career after completing his studies at the National Autonomous University of Mexico in 1954. Before ever designing houses, his interests focused on the history of architecture, which he taught for some time. He was very impressed by pre-Columbian Mexican architecture, with its geometry and monumental appearance; many similar qualities were highlighted by 1950s and 1960s brutalism. In his own work, he connected both to create a unique version of expressive concrete architecture with bold forms, huge concrete surfaces, and sharp angles. In 1968, he debuted a new building for the Folkloric Ballet School in Mexico City, which was founded by his sister Amalia Hernández, a world-renowned choreographer. Hernández became her brother's client again in 1970, when she commissioned him to design her family's private residence. She came up with a striking design solution for the home, which became one of Hernández Navarro's most celebrated works. A pure celebration of sculptural form, the house is inspired by dynamism in movement and dance. The

huge concrete volumes create an unconventional structure, with round vaults on the street side of the property and sharp edges oriented toward the garden. Among the most exciting features in the interior are sculptural organic stairs, twisted in the middle of the liquid-looking space, and a futurist corridor framed by huge circular openings. After the completion of Casa Amalia Hernández, the architect continued to design breathtaking structures, including the Mexican Pavilion at the Expo 1970 in Osaka, Japan, the Heroic Military College in Mexico, with the form of a robotic face, and his own studio and house shaped like an elevated Mexican pyramid. (STE)

fig. b   fig. c (opposite page)

fig. d

Two of Agustín Hernández Navarro's striking
projects were built for his sister, choreographer Amalia
Hernández, who commissioned this house in 1970.

AGUSTÍN HERNÁNDEZ NAVARRO CASA AMALIA HERNÁNDEZ

fig. d & e: Round
shapes meet sharp and
hard edges in this
exceptional example
of Mexican brutalism.
The living room also
features a sculptural
fireplace.

fig. f: The monumental
geometry is counter-
acted broken with the
sensual forms of the
staircase.

Maison Unal

Architect: Claude Häusermann-Costy & Joël Unal
Location: Ardèche, France
Completion date: 1976

Les maisons bulles, or French bubble houses, of the 1960s and 1970s evoke a futurism that continues to resonate loudly to this day.

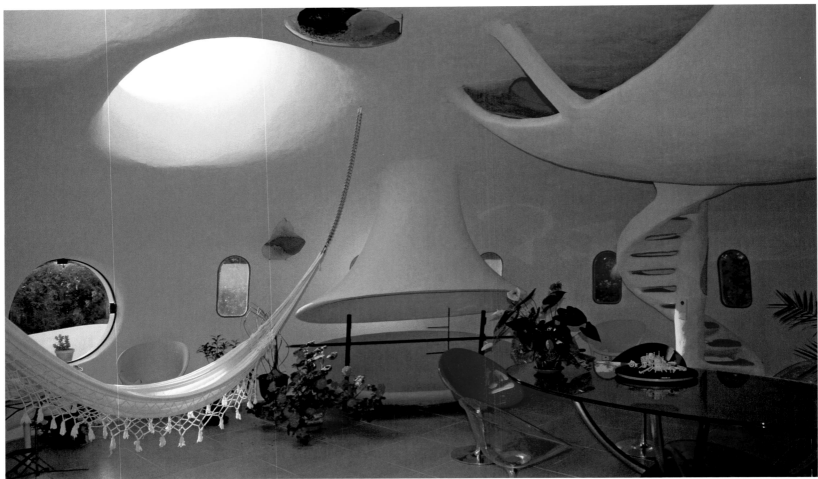

fig. a

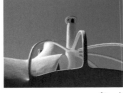

fig. b

fig. a, d, e & f: Using reinforced concrete allowed the architect to create entire structures as single-piece forms.

fig. b & c: Set within a natural forested setting, the organic form of the house is said to represent fungi.

The concrete spheres of Maison Unal create an interior that sits in a charming world somewhere between the handmade and the futuristic. This maison bulle, or bubble house, became something of a type in France during the 1960s. In the immediate postwar period, the concept of mass housing dominated, such that when architects designed single houses they had to present them as prototypes for mass production. In the 1960s this was met with resistance. Influenced by Antoni Gaudí or Frederick Kiesler, and inspired by nature, architects of the time elected to create singular self-built houses. Claude Häusermann-Costy may have been the ostensible designer of Maison Unal, but the client, Joël Unal, was the co-designer and primary builder.

From the exterior, the house is experienced as a series of geometric shapes deployed in a rocky landscape. The interiors are a different matter altogether—womb-like and intimate, yet still dramatic in their curvaceous extravagance. Maison Unal is perhaps the most important early example of a particularly popular technique in France, a mélange of craft and industrial processes. The home is constructed from concrete poured into hand-built, metal formwork on site, resulting in an emphasis on the building as a sculpture.

The inhabitable 200-square-meter work of art is composed of three particularly large spaces: a dining room, a library, and a workshop. Connected to and above these spaces are the bedrooms and kitchen. Shelves are integrated into the structures, constructed either from the same process of handmade reinforced concrete or from wood. Unlike other maisons bulles, this house is raised above the ground, allowing natural light to pass from beneath the spherical room as well as from above, with warm sunlight diffusing through the cave-like spaces. (ABR)

fig. c   fig. d (opposite page)

fig. e

CLAUDE HÄUSERMANN-COSTY & JOËL UNAL MAISON UNAL

fig. g & h: Color and form including round windows are paramount. Spaces are defined by a change in color, while a number of features, shelving, for example, are built in.

fig. f

fig. g

fig. h

Preserver of the Lanzarote Horizon

CÉSAR MANRIQUE

* June 24, 1919, Arrecife, Lanzarote, Canary Islands
† September 25, 1992 (aged 73), São Paulo, Brazil

Lanzarote, among the beautiful Canary Islands, became witness to the tireless creative passion of local artist and architect César Manrique. Between the late 1960s and early 1990s, Manrique designed many notable projects here, forever changing the landscape of this island.

Manrique was born in 1919 in the city of Arrecife on Lanzarote. He fought voluntarily in the Spanish Civil War in the artillery unit on Franco's side. After the war, he enrolled at University of La Laguna to study architecture, but never finished. In 1945 he moved to Madrid and received a scholarship for the Art School of San Fernando, where he graduated as a teacher of art and painting. ▷

ARRIETA WINDMILL

Manrique's work is deeply entwined with the makeup of his homeland. For example, his windmills present a visual reminder of the trade winds that characterize the island's climate.

213

In the middle of the 1960s he traveled to New York, where he stayed for three years due to a grant from Nelson Rockefeller's fund. His own artistic style evolved during that time, and his colorful abstract paintings served as a prelude to later artistic and architectural projects on Lanzarote. At the end of his stay in New York, he exhibited his works at the prestigious Catherine Viviano Gallery, which earned him an international reputation.

He returned to Lanzarote with cosmopolitan, modern sensibilities, which had a major influence on local planning regulations. Manrique recognized the potential of tourism on the island, and successfully lobbied to encourage natural and non-aggressive development of this industry while still respecting the volcanic habitat of the island. He fought against the idea of high-rise hotels in favor of preserving the natural beauty of the island. He stipulated that all new buildings must use traditional colors in their exterior decorations, which also strongly influenced his own work.

When he returned from New York, he began working on his own house, manifesting his architectural style for the first time

TARO DE TACHICHE

Location: Lanzarote, Canary Islands
Completion date: 1968

Ultra-modern, brilliant white floors and furnishings sit within the caverns of Lanzarote's ancient volcanic terrain. The result is an extraordinary blend of loft-style living within an untamed-nature environment. Manrique had allowed the landscape to dictate space rather than the other way around.

JAMEOS DEL AGUA

Location: Lanzarote, Canary Islands
Completion date: 1966

Manrique's underground entertainment complex is unique in its exploitation of its natural surroundings—a *jameo* is a volcanic cave whose roof has collapsed. Visitors can swim in a lake with the clearest water, while musicians play in a cavelike environment in which the acoustics are said to be incredible.

in the natural landscape and setting the stage for his later work. Located on the site of Lanzarote's eighteenth-century volcanic eruptions, the home's majestic 3,000-square-meter lot is tucked into the rocky landscape. The ground-level rooms of the clean white building, including his studio space, are influenced by traditional Lanzarote style, while also made modern with open spaces and large windows.

"For me Lanzarote was the most beautiful place on Earth."
César Manrique

The most interesting part of the house is hidden beneath the volcanic rocks. The basement, covered by a natural roof of volcanic bubbles, contains five living areas sculpted into the basalt. The central cave houses a ▷

JAMEOS DEL AGUA

> "If people could see Lanzarote through my eyes, they'd think the same as me."
> *César Manrique*

in 1966, are part of a subterranean series of entertainment spaces that include a concert hall, two dance floors, three bars, an underground lake filled with blind albino crabs, a swimming pool, and a museum about volcanism. The natural architecture collides with strong brutalist-inspired organic forms.

In 1992, Manrique died in a car accident at Tahíche, Teguise, very near his Lanzarote home. He was 73 years old. But his legacy remains. The Manrique House, as well as his other projects, are preserved thanks to a foundation he set up in his name in 1982 along with a group of friends. Based at Manrique's home, the foundation is a private, non-profit organization that helps to preserve local nature and architecture while allowing tourists to enjoy the views.   (STE)

JARDIN DE CACTUS

Location: Lanzarote, Canary Islands
Completion date: 1990

This disused quarry was an inspired choice for César Manrique's final project—a beautifully landscaped botanical garden. What were once the manmade steps of the quarry are now terraces planted with more than 1,000 species of cacti, reached through a series of interwoven paths that link the different areas and levels.

lounge area with a swimming pool, barbecue, and small dance floor. Manrique succeeded in creating a breathtaking space, where the artificial meets the natural in a beautiful symbiosis. The interior also includes custom-made stone benches and corners for lounging that look like they have come straight out of a James Bond film. The house has been preserved in its original splendor and serves as an exciting tourist destination. Visitors can walk around the building and enjoy great tapas and drinks served by waiters in Manrique-designed uniforms.

In addition to his house, Manrique designed many other exceptional projects around the island. All of them connect the natural volcanic landscape and traditional island architecture with the artist's endless imagination. Jameos del Agua and Casa de los Volcanes, built

Palais Bulles

Architect: Antti Lovag
Location: Théoule-sur-Mer, France
Completion date: 1989

From the outside, the organic forms of this remarkable home resemble bubbling lava. On the inside, the rooms play host to a space-age extravaganza.

fig. a

fig. a & g: Built on the rocky outcrop of a volcanic mountain range, the house offers vistas overlooking the Mediterranean Sea.

fig. b: The building's terra-cotta exterior blends in with the red tones of the volcanic rock on which it sits.

fig. c: Almost all of the forms within the building—beds, alcoves, and decorative details—are curvaceous.

The *maison bulle* phenomenon emerged from a particularly French approach to self-build homes in the 1960s. The style of building—*voile de béton*—permits the hand-making of spherical spaces intersected by great swoops of sculptural concrete. Many of these houses were built by architects working closely with clients who built the substructure of iron rebar work. This gave each home a charming and singular combination of futuristic shapes and roughly textured handmade forms. Palais Bulles, with its view back toward Cannes, is of a different order, however. Slowly built between 1975 and 1989 by the late Hungarian architect Antti Lovag, who described himself as a "habitologist," it was commissioned by the industrialist Pierre Bernard; Lovag had previously built another home for Bernard on the Mediterranean coast. Palais Bulles was then bought

by Pierre Cardin in 1992. With the guidance of Lovag, Cardin expanded it into a kind of uber party-grotto, featuring ten rooms, three swimming pools, and an adjacent amphitheater.

Cardin insisted that the curves of the house represented femininity, but for Lovag the circle was not only symbolic of a pleasing shape, but also a means of reproducing a primitive conviviality. In an added twist, Cardin commissioned contemporary artists such as Patrice Breteau and Gérard Le Cloarec to create immersive artistic environments in each of the ten rooms. Breteau's cosmological surrealism is particularly suited to the spherical environment. Rather than using the uniformly soft, fleshy tones of earlier maisons bulles, Palais Bulles is painted in strong colors and finished with ingenious bespoke benches and soft furniture. The procession through the space is also much clearer, which is helpful given that, on top of the parties, the house also played host to the occasional catwalk show—not just for its owner but for other fashion houses too. (ABR)

fig. b   fig. c (opposite page)   fig. d (following double page)

ANTTI LOVAG PALAIS BULLES

fig. e

fig. f

fig. d: The chairs and sofas that fill the rooms have biomorphic forms reminiscent of plants and flowers.

fig. e: This sculptural egg, featured inside an alcove, is designed by Patrice Breteau. His signature is visible above.

fig. f: Stepping into the red bedroom with its metallic wall finishes is like finding yourself at the center of the Earth.

fig. g

Grataloup Apartment

This dreamy, cavernous apartment in Geneva epitomises the utopian ideals of the 1970s Organic and Sculptural Movement.

Architect: Daniel Grataloup
Location: Geneva, Switzerland
Completion date: 1968

French/Swiss architect Daniel Grataloup has lived in his spacious apartment since 1968, which sits on the fifth floor of a residential block designed by architect André Gaillard. He had problems building his own house when he first arrived in Geneva from France, so he bought this apartment and adapted it with his wife, sculptress Diana Schley. With precision, he entirely redecorated the rationalist apartment according to his principles of organic architecture.

The living room is full of complex scenery, a rock that naturally grows with the individual and current needs of its inhabitants. The gypsum walls are full of niches, shelves, and overhangs. The fiberglass seating modules have built-in headphone connectors and integrated speakers are all around— perfect for the parties that Grataloup hosted. The dining room is completely paneled with copper sheets, creating an irregular relief decor. A monumental metal table dominates the middle of the room. One of Grataloup's models of a utopic 1970s residential tower stands in the corner, part of an archive that the Museum of Modern Art in New York acquired for their permanent collection in 2012.

fig. a   fig. b (opposite page)

fig. a, b, & d: Daniel Grataloup adapted this rigid modernist apartment with his organic inventions. His apartment is built into the classic housing block.

Copper is not the only material the architect used to panel the walls of his home. Various decorative elements are made out of lead, cork, plastic, wood, gypsum, and textile. Grataloup's own oil paintings are built into the walls in some places. The apartment is somehow subversive, a parasite on the modernist purity of the residential block from the 1960s. This is evident on the exterior as well, where the architect rounded all of the windows to contrast with the purism. The interior is an artificial cave where one continually finds bizarre artistic or functional traces of this dreamer of architecture without right angles.   (STE)

The spacious living room is full of complex scenery,
a rock that naturally grows with the changing needs of
its inhabitants.

fig. c

fig. d

fig. e

fig. f

fig. c: The dining room features a massive copper table and sculptural copper plates that cover the walls.

fig. e: Grataloup even changed the dimensions and shapes of the classic rectangular windows.

DISCOVERING POETRY IN PRAGMATISM

— *Leme House* by Paolo Mendes da Rocha,
pp. 258–265

Casa de Vidro

Architect: Lina Bo Bardi
Location: São Paulo, Brazil
Completion date: 1951

One of the best Brazilian modernist houses is hidden in the middle of lush, tropical jungle. Architect Lina Bo Bardi created a subtle glass structure, forever changing the relationship between inside and out.

fig. a

fig. a: The outside vegetation creates a natural background for the sleek modernist design inside the house, which is characterized by complete transparency.

fig. b: The house, which was originally built on the vast land, is now owned by the Bo Bardi's foundation, which opens the villa to the public a few days per week.

Among the famous architects of the second half of the last century in Brazil is Italian architect and designer Lina Bo Bardi. Her architectural career started in her homeland Italy in the early 1940s, where she collaborated with Gio Ponti and wrote for magazines such as *Stile, Grazia, Belleza,* and *Domus.* In 1946, she moved from Milan to Rome and married collector and curator Pietro Maria Bardi.

In 1951, when Bo Bardi and her husband became official citizens of Brazil, they started to build their own house. Her Casa de Vidro (Glass House) in the Morumbi district of São Paulo is one of the most important works of postwar modernism, representing the fusion of European rationalism and South American creative temperament. Lightness and transparency borrowed from the Bauhaus principles of modern architecture connect with newer elements coming from the tropical climate and expressive natural forms of Brazil. The one-story structure is elevated above the ground by thin subtle pillars to create a living platform, floating above the tropical vegetation. The central staircase, situated in the home's courtyard, leads to the open interior. The façade of the house consists of floor-to-ceiling walls on all sides, giving way to a greenhouse-like atmosphere that allows nature in. The form of the interior follows Mies van der Rohe's philosophy of open-plan living, furnished with Bo Bardi's own designs, as well as historical pieces and rare artifacts from around the world. Here, rational architecture meets the rich sensuality of the lush environment. Casa de Vidro has attracted wider attention from the global art and architecture community in recent years. Prestigious magazines have profiled the house on their pages, and companies and curators are fascinated by the authentic atmosphere of the house. While Hans Ulrich Obrist curated an artistic installation inside the house, companies such as Izé and Arper have relaunched some of Bo Bardi's designs. (STE)

fig. b   fig. c (opposite page)

Bo Bardi's Casa de Vidro in São Paulo is one of the
most important works of postwar modernism, representing
the fusion of European rationalism and South American
creative temperament.

fig. c: The interior of
the house was designed
around the central
rectangular atrium.

fig. d & g: The main
living room was
designed according
to the philosophy
of free-flowing open
space, an important
concept of the modern-
ist movement.

fig. e: The kitchen is
simple and efficient,
with no unnecessary
decoration.

fig. f: Lina Bo Bardi
was very interested
in folk art, which she
mixed with her own
furniture pieces in
the interior.

fig. f   fig. g (following double page)

The Modernist
of São Paulo

VILANOVA ARTIGAS

* June 23, 1915, Curitiba, Brazil
† January 12, 1985 (aged 69), São Paulo, Brazil

The story of modern architecture in Brazil is written by several phenomenally creative individuals who adapted the European modernist ideology of the 1920s to the tropical climate of South America. One of them was João Batista Vilanova Artigas, an architect of huge gestures and endless creative power. Artigas is one of the most important figures of São Paulo's postwar architectural scene, a scene that also included Paulo Mendes da Rocha, Lina Bo Bardi, Joaquim Guedes, and Rino Levi. Together they created the powerful Paulista school of architecture, which became dominant during the 1950s and 1960s after the rise of Rio de Janeiro's Carioca school in the 1940s and

"The city is a house
and the house is a city."
Vilanova Artigas

early 1950s. Artigas is, next to Paulo Mendes da Rocha, the most important figure of the Brazilian brutalist movement. Influenced by the seminal figures of modern architecture, he developed a striking signature style based on the use of dynamic volumes and strong shapes, which he applied to both important public commissions and private residences. His

designs are unorthodox masterpieces in regard to colors, surfaces, light, and space.

Artigas was born in 1915 in Curitiba in the state of Paraná. His initial training was as an engineer, but he later graduated as an architect from the Polytechnic School of the University of São Paulo in 1937. He was fortunate to collaborate with the pioneers of the Brazilian modern movement soon after, ▷

BAETA HOUSE

Location: São Paulo, Brazil
Completion date: 1957

Artigas created large open spaces with great transparency so that one level was visible from another and the outside merged with the inside. Originally, the walls were colored according to their structural hierarchy: blue for load-bearing walls and columns; red and yellow for non-load-bearing.

first with Oswaldo Bratke and then Gregori Warchavchik, who is often credited for designing the first modernist Brazilian home in 1928. Artigas's first domestic projects were heavily influenced by Frank Lloyd Wright. His first house, built in 1942, and the Rio Branco Paranhos House, completed one year later, evoke the formal vocabulary of Wright's organic architecture.

In the mid-1940s, he co-founded the São Paulo wing of the Brazilian Institute of Architects. He then left for the United States

"I admire the poets. What they say with two words we have to express with thousands of bricks."
Vilanova Artigas

Location: São Paulo,
Brazil
Completion date: 1957

Rubens de Mendonça House
is also known as the
"House of Triangles,"
owing to Francisco
Rebolo Gonzales's strik-
ing blue and white fres-
co on the façade. The
building is an exercise
in geometry through and
through, with the trian-
gle motif repeating in
structural elements as
well as decorative ones.

on a Guggenheim Fellowship, where he met several European architects and visited Frank Lloyd Wright's houses. As Artigas grew into his own expressive style at the end of the 1940s, he began to redevelop the pitched overhanging roofs and horizontal character of his buildings. His 1949 Czapski House, with its sloping roof, demonstrates a more tectonically rigorous attitude toward the articulation of structural form—a signature of the Paulista school. He also designed his second private residence with these sharp-edged forms that same year. A completely glazed pavilion is covered by a sloping butterfly roof, covering an interior with intermediate levels. A similar structure defines his later residential and public works. Ramps, dynamic slopes, diamond-shaped pillars, and dramatic indoor spaces characterize his

landmark projects, such as the 1952 Londrina Bus Station, the 1961 Santa Paula Yacht Club, the 1962 Guarulhos High School, and the celebrated Faculty of Architecture and Urbanism at the University of São Paulo, built between 1961 and 1968. ▷

This last project is the true gem of São Paulo's Paulista school. The huge mass of concrete sits on subtle triangular-shaped pilotis, a stark juxtapositon with the monumentality of the material. The interior of the structure is dominated by a central open space, avoiding divisions and hierarchy. The six floors are connected by a series of ramps that lend an integrity and continuity to the space. The interior of the building became famous through photographs that show it packed with students demonstrating against the military regime.

Despite becoming a prolific architect working on huge public projects, Artigas was increasingly preoccupied with the potential for a single structural form to embody an entire program, irrespective of the size and status of the commission. A private house became a playground for experimentation. Baeta House in São Paulo, completed in 1957, is the first of his residential masterpieces. The house rests on six columns with cantilevers supported by ties. The residence, built for Olga Baeta, has ▷

ARTIGAS RESIDENCE

Location: São Paulo, Brazil
Completion date: 1949

With its facade turned away from the street, the Vilanova Artigas residence is raised on pilotis at one end and the roofline slopes to single-story level at the other. A glazed corridor runs the entire width—and height—of this space. As in other works, the walls are color-coded according to their function.

> "If forms are absurd, it is because
> the premises are irrational."
> *Vilanova Artigas*

intermediate levels. The architect also used triangular-shaped pillars in this project for the first time, a design that gave the building, together with its abstract mural, the name House of Triangles.

Probably the most dramatic of Artigas's 1950s houses is the second Taques Bittencourt House, completed in 1959. The residence unfolds vertically as a sequence of floors at intermediate levels, with areas of differing ceiling heights. Instead of stairs, the architect used longitudinal ramps to connect floors. Artigas arranged the rooms in an unusual layout, with service areas at the front of the house behind the massive stone wall and living areas at the back. The interior space is arranged around

ELZA BERQUÓ HOUSE

Location: São Paulo, Brazil
Completion date: 1967

Artigas's interpretation of the brutalist style that became a feature of modern architecture from 1950–1970 is almost oppressive. The extrerior seating area with is "broken" raw concrete enclosure has the atmosphere of a bunker. Ceiling heights feel low and give the rooms a subterranean feel—an effect that is emphasized by the fact that the main light sources come from a hole cut into the heavy, flat roof.

floors at intermediate levels, a variety of ceiling heights, and a studio—features the architect had already begun employing in his second private house. The dramatic living room space has varied levels and opens into the garden through an extensive glass wall. The architect also divided and characterized different sections of the interior using bright colors, including red, yellow, and blue. The 1959 Rubens de Mendonça House has a similar arrangement of space. The house, whose façade is painted with a triangular op-art-like abstract mural, is organized as a vertical sequence of

a central atrium with lush tropical vegetation. During the 1960s, Artigas changed his spatial approach to private space. In his residential projects—including the 1963 Ivo Viterito House, the Mendes André House, built between 1966 and 1967—and the 1967 Elza Berquó House, he redefined the relationship between an expression of forces and a minimization of the supporting structure. In these designs, he created a new type of residential structure similar to Paulo Mendes da Rocha's houses, which later became a model for São Paulo's brutalist homes.

Elza Berquó House is the finest example of this approach and another shining example of the Paulista school. Its exposed brutalist structure has come a long way from the midcentury colorful, elegant shapes of the architect's postwar houses. The change in style also represents a change in the political climate. Artigas was very worried about the

future of the country under the new repressive military dictatorship, which even landed him under judicial investigation. The raw concrete structure of the house is supported by pieces of tree trunks as interior pillars. As if a livable bunker lit by a series of roof skylights and patios, the space reflects the brutality of the time, as well as a new architectural language of the late 1960s. （STE）

Vandenhaute-Kiebooms House

Architect: Juliaan Lampens
Location: Huise, Belgium
Completion date: 1967

Regional Belgian architect Juliaan Lampens dedicated his career to envisioning unconventional ways of everyday living. His Vandenhaute-Kiebooms House highlights a radical open-plan family structure.

fig. a

fig. a: The open-space interior is divided by just a few fixed elements and walls, including these cylinders for the bathroom and stairs.

fig. b: From outside, the house looks like a simple cube with its massive concrete roof and floor-to-ceiling windows.

Juliaan Lampens's architectural work was largely unknown before it was recently revisited on the pages of prominent architecture and design magazines. The Belgian brutalist was a great admirer of Le Corbusier and Oscar Niemeyer, and a study of his sculptural villas from the 1960s and 1970s uncover influences from both modern architecture masters, manifested in an unexpected and surprising symbiosis.

Lampens's buildings connect French Le Corbusier's structural and material brutality with Brazilian Niemeyer's formal poesy and sculptural sensibility. Two of his most impressive and expressive house designs demonstrate his application of both approaches: one for teacher Gerard Vandenhaute in 1967, the other for professor Albert Van Wassenhove in 1974.

While the Van Wassenhove House is now open to the public for guided tours, as well as for overnight stays, the Vandenhaute-Kiebooms House is still a private residence. The latter is the finest implementation of the radical spatial and social avant-garde ideas of the architect, who at the time was based in the small village of Eke on the outskirts of Ghent. His idea was to create an open-plan living room, which privileges community and equality within the space over a bourgeois insistence on individuality and patriarchy. The house, constructed of a massive exposed concrete and glass façade, was built on an exact 14 × 14 meter square, creating an absolute openness in the interior. Here, a family with four children could live together without any visual and acoustic privacy. Lampens created a playful interior landscape with various screens and walls to divide the space into different functional zones and corners. This includes a sculptural kitchen space, separated only by concrete semi-walls suspended from the ceiling. The only fixed elements in the interior include three concrete cylinders that hide a bath, toilet, and the stairs to the cellar. The cylinders rise from the floor to the height of Gerard Vandenhaute, an enlightened client who had no fear of experimentation. (STE)

fig. b

fig. c

fig. c: One of the most striking ways to divide the space can be seen by these walls suspended from the ceiling.

fig. d: Juliaan Lampens was truly a sculptural architect, designing ordinary elements as sculptures, as is evident in this rain dripstone.

Casa Butantã

Architect: Paolo Mendes da Rocha
Location: São Paulo, Brazil
Completion date: 1966

A principal example of the celebrated Paulista School of Architecture, Paolo Mendes da Rocha's Casa Butantã is a masterclass in austerity and brutality of form and space.

While Oscar Niemeyer was the master of the Rio de Janeiro–based Carioca school of Brazilian architectural modernism, Pritzker Prize winner Paulo Mendes da Rocha was the leader of the competing Paulista school, originating in the concrete jungle of São Paulo. During the 1950s, he invented his own

Mendes da Rocha's own residence. Consisting of two almost identical houses built next to each other, the residential structure was designed by the architect for himself and his sister. As a Communist, he wanted to create an avant-garde statement to strongly contrast with the mainstream decorative style of this middle-class neighborhood. The biggest weapon in his fight was exposed concrete, from which he constructed elevated residential structures with a large overhanging roof and sun protectors.

Completed in 1966, the twin house seems to float above the ground. The main living space is situated on the first floor above a hollow space used for parking. The space is accessed by an external staircase that creates an impressive sculptural element. The open living room is framed by a long narrow line of windows in the subtle steel casing. The floor is covered by traditional azulejos, or decorative Portuguese tiles—their rich historical character contrasts with the exposed concrete both in and outside the house. Like a domestic, walk-in refrigerator, the floor protects its inhabitants from the tropical climate beyond. (STE)

fig. a

elaborate version of tropical brutalism, using exposed concrete surfaces and striking sculptural forms. Mendes da Rocha rejected the organic fluidity and elegant lightweight forms of the Carioca school, and instead began to design houses as compact concrete boxes, using a huge mass of material to protect their interiors from strong sun and high humidity.

The finest example of this movement is a series of private houses built by Mendes da Rocha around Sao Paulo's metropolitan area in the 1960s. One of these homes, located in the Butantã district, also served as

fig. b

fig. a, b, d, & e: Paulo Mendes da Rocha created a striking contrast between the mass of concrete and the slender lines of the windows in his residence.

fig. c: Exposed concrete was the primary material for São Paulo architects of the 1960s.

fig. c

fig. f: The dining
room of Mendes da
Rocha's house has a
limited and subtle
color palette of gray
concrete and brown
hardwood, used for
furniture.

fig. e   fig. f (following double page)

fig. g, h, & i: Mendes
da Rocha complemented
the roughness of con-
crete with industrial-
looking designs and
his own custom-made
pieces.

fig. g

fig. h

fig. i

Pritzker Prize winner Paulo Mendes da Rocha
was the leader of São Paulo's Paulista school, creating
a material poetry from exposed concrete.

Leme House

Architect: Paolo Mendes da Rocha
Location: São Paulo, Brazil
Completion date: 1970

The gallery-like space of the Leme House celebrates raw exposed concrete at its best, allowing modesty and simplicity to meet monumentality in the domestic space.

fig. a

fig. a & d: The two-story living space of the residence doubles as a private domestic gallery.

fig. b: Strict elementary geometry was one of the strongest creative forces of Brazilian brutalist architects, as seen on the staircases above the pool.

fig. c: Nothing but the pure form of concrete with marks from the wooden casing creates the beauty of Brazilian modernism.

Paulo Mendes da Rocha was the most influential Brazilian architect in São Paulo during the 1970s. Beginning in the early 1960s, he built several private residences into which he introduced raw exposed concrete. One of the most extreme implementations of concrete in the domestic space can be seen in the Eduardo Leme House, originally built in 1970 for Fernando Millan. Built in São Paulo, the house keeps the rectangular proportions that Mendes da Rocha used in his series of previous houses, including the Mario Masetti House and his twin Butantã houses. The sectors of the house are arranged from a central void that absorbs the stairs and the walkway. In this case, there are no pilotis and the house is half-buried in a steep site. On the first floor, the private sector's bathroom and the social sector's bathroom are integrated into the central elements, receiving direct lighting and ventilation from the exterior. They fragment the suggestion of an open-plan design, where the living room and the bedrooms are modularly inserted.

The interior of the house, lit mainly from above by a series of skylights, has a gallery-like appearance. The central living room is far from a cozy living space. With its round concrete staircase in the middle and no windows on the sidewalls, one can feel as though they are in cold storage. Furnished with icons of modern design, the space is actually a private gallery. The current owner of the house, art collector and gallerist Eduardo Leme, equipped the space with an exquisite selection of paintings and sculptures, highlighting the brutality of the used concrete background. He also furnished the space with icons of Brazilian and international modernist design. The geometrical austerity of the house complements the qualities of Gerrit Rietveld's Utrecht Armchair, as well as the extravagant leather and steel wire chairs, designed by Brazilian architect and artist Flávio de Carvalho and produced by French furniture company Objekto. Leme also commissioned Mendes da Rocha to design his own gallery building in 2012. (STE)

fig. b   fig. c (opposite page)   fig. d (following double page)

fig. e

PAOLO MENDES DA ROCHA <u>LEME HOUSE</u>

fig. e: Today, the house is furnished with icons of twentieth-century design such as Gerrit Rietveld's Utrecht Armchair.

fig. f & g: Above the main living space, the architect designed a series of walkways and galleries.

fig. h: Wooden built-in desks create practical work stations in the children's room.

fig. i: The bathroom resembles the modesty and austerity of a monk's cell.

fig. j: The house is owned by Eduardo Leme, an art collector and gallerist who uses it to showcase his extensive collection.

fig. i

PAOLO MENDES DA ROCHA   LEME HOUSE

One of the most extreme implementations of concrete in the private living space is seen in the Eduardo Leme House, originally built in 1970 for Fernando Millan.

Rebberg House

Architect: Hans Demarmel
Location: Zurich, Switzerland
Completion date: 1965

The brutalist architecture of the 1950s to 1970s had a futuristic edge to it, but some felt it offered a dystopian view of the world rather than a utopian one.

fig. a

fig. a & b: The structure of the building and its various functions are inseparable; the staircase, for instance, is built into the fireplace.

fig. c, d, & f: Color is limited in this interior design, and is most often used to define spaces, as the orange ceiling does for the kitchen/dining area.

fig. e & g: The chaise-longue by Eames is one of the few concessions to comfort here; surfaces are harsh and purely functional rather than decorative.

Brutalism was, to some extent, a reaction to the style dubbed "soft" modernism that had long dominated European and American midcentury design. It was also a reaction to the expense of it. As such, brutal architecture made use of raw concrete. Not only was the material deemed the most honest for letting a structure speak for itself, but also relatively cheap to use. It became the material of choice for government and municipal buildings, and for large social-housing projects—making it essentially utopian in its outlook. It should be noted that brutalism does not relate to the word "brutal" in the harsh, oppressive sense that some critics promote, but stems from the French term *béton brut*, coined by Le Corbusier, which simply means raw concrete.

And whose concept also arrived in Suisse: Hans Demarmels's Rebberg House in Zurich was conceived as one of three modular blocks, their structures locking together like teeth in a jigsaw. It is built on a steep incline and its form reflects this. The floors of the building are staggered to accommodate the slope of the land, and the façade features a collection of strong geometric shapes—protrusions, terraces, and pergolas that emphasize the ways in which the building functions within, while also interacting with its exterior surroundings. The interior rooms of the building are set on seven half-floors around a central staircase. In tune with classical modernist theory, this unique design allows spaces to flow horizontally and vertically; the vistas within the building are not just linear, but also vertical. Structures inside the building mirror those of its façade. Strong geometric shapes abound. The eye is drawn to the sculptural fireplace in the living room or the kitchen island with its recessed features. It makes for a very dynamic interior. (SOU)

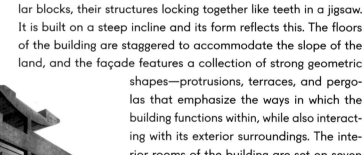

fig. b   fig. c (opposite page)

In tune with classical modernist theory, the
Rebberg House's unique design allows spaces to flow
horizontally and vertically; the vistas within the building
are not just linear, but also vertical.

fig. e

fig. f

fig. g

Marlene Milan House

Architect: Marcos Acayaba
Location: São Paulo, Brazil
Completion date: 1975

The drama of this interior is created by the juxtaposition of a luscious curved roof with the taut, well-considered layout of the rectilinear rooms.

fig. a

fig. a: The dramatic reinforced concrete roof is effectively a bridge between two sides of a narrow channel.

fig. b: Underneath a flight of concrete stairs, a Le Corbusier chaise longue evokes the sweeping roof above.

fig. b

The Marlene Milan House, built in 1975, came at a key moment in the evolution of a uniquely Brazilian domestic architecture. It was inspired not only by the surrounding hills of the Cidade Jardim, which rise above the city grid of São Paulo, but also by the curvaceous buildings of Brazil's modernist titans such as Oscar Niemeyer.

The house is dominated by a sweeping concrete roof that enfolds the living spaces, divided across two floors within. The floor plan makes use of the varying ground levels of the original terrain to create three separate but connected platforms. With an open-plan living space at the center, the space is reminiscent of the western U.S. modernist homes of the 1950s and 1960s. A dining area, kitchen, and service space sit on a lower level, while the bedrooms are placed on a slightly raised level. The undulating roof ensures that the whole building is visually connected, not just internally but also in tying the tropical gardens at both ends of the house to the interior space. Internally, the extraordinary beauty derives from the contrast between the rectilinear design of the house's living spaces and the rolling roof form; externally, its beauty grows out of a relationship with the thick plantings in the garden. There is a constant interplay between the exterior and interior, enhanced by a selection of materials that are suitable for both environments. The red tiles of the pool terrace continue into the living space. Bespoke furniture, such as a huge concrete-framed banquette and bookcase, keep the space clear of clutter.

The house was first designed for Acayaba's sister-in-law, the psychoanalyst and writer Betty Milan, who had no strong brief but wanted four bedrooms, a long swimming pool, and a photography studio. But as the project came to completion, Acayaba's client decided to leave Brazil, so the architect himself moved into the house. He and his wife—Marlene—have made good use of the house since living there. For instance, the photo lab, hidden under the elevated poolside terrace, has been put to good use as a studio.　(ABR)

fig. c

fig. c & g: The living
room interior is a
canny juxtaposition of
an in-built bookshelf
and a banquette with
an open plan and full
length glazing.

fig. d: Originally
a dark room for the
client, this space has
been converted into a
studio.

fig. e: The internal
structure is artful.
Here the stairs are
augmented by a steel
screen inlaid with
colourful paneling.

fig. d   fig. e (following double page)

Internally, the beauty derives from the contrast between the rectilinear design of the house's living spaces and the rolling roof form; externally, its beauty grows out of a relationship with the thick plantings in the garden.

MARCOS ACAYABA

MARLENE MILAN HOUSE

fig. f

fig. g

fig. f: The long
horizontal window
with inbuilt parallel
counter accentuates
the length of the
kitchen.

fig. h: To collapse the
distinction between
interior and exterior,
plantings have been
introduced within the
building.

fig. h

Tomie Ohtake House

Dominated by a single space that is part-gallery, part-home, but all brutalist, this is an artist's house unafraid to possess its own singular aesthetic power.

Architect: Ruy Ohtake
Location: São Paulo, Brazil
Completion date: 1968

The work of Japanese-born artist Tomie Ohtake is familiar to anyone who visits the state of São Paolo; be it her sensual tapestry for the interior of the Memorial da América Latina or the striking red-and-steel oculus on the Avenida Paulista. The artist arrived in Brazil in 1936 and became a celebrated figure in abstract art. Her São Paulo home is a severe, even brutalist structure designed in the 1960s by her son, architect Ruy Ohtake. The house was designed as an austere backdrop to his mother's work and personality, wonderfully showcasing her extravagant, colorful paintings and sculptures.

The living section of the home is ferociously simple. Stretching out in front of visitors as they arrive, it has the quality of an industrial shed. Defined by a series of cross beams placed every meter, which are supported on the side walls, this part of the house is unencumbered by columns or inter-

fig. a   fig. b (opposite page)   fig. c (following double page)

fig. a: The concrete plate which forms the bulk of this building's structure is curved in welcome on approach.

fig. b: Huge cross beams would dominate this main space were it not for the bright bedroom pavilions beneath.

fig. c: The eclectically decorated study which stands off the main space merges into the enclosed garden beyond.

nal walls. Any divisions that do exist are solely to break up the long space and provide the owner with private areas. This ostensibly private section of the house is effectively populated by a number of discrete pavilions. These are created by walls of concrete painted in bright primary colors, delimiting spaces like the kitchen and bedrooms. Elsewhere, fixed shelving and bespoke furniture is sited in concrete recesses. At the heart of the long space is a curved table.

Even with this nominally private part of the home, the building is essentially a 750-square-meter lived-in gallery for exhibiting Ohtake's vibrant work. And in the more public wing of the house to the left of the entryway, the dining room sits among a set-piece of the artist's studio, a library, and a room dedicated to her own collection. The garden, which takes up the final quarter of the building, is legible as a courtyard within the larger complex, framed by the windows within the building. (ABR)

Even with the private parts of the home, the
building is essentially a 750-square-meter lived-in gallery
for exhibiting Tomie Ohtake's vibrant work.

fig. d

fig. d: The study is continuous with a workshop: vital space given how unwieldy Ohtake's sculptures as the metalpipes beyond the skylight often are.

fig. e & f: The real charm of the house is in the way that the monumental spaces are divided up—here by delicate partitions. And in the artful furnishing such as the massive concrete dining table in the eating area.

The Mexican Minimalist with an Eye for Color

LUIS BARRAGÁN

* March 9, 1902, Guadalajara, Mexico
† November 22, 1988 (aged 86), Mexico City, Mexico

Experimental work with color, space, and volumes meets vernacular inspiration in the work of Luis Barragán, the most influential Mexican architect of the twentieth century. The only Mexican to win the Pritzker Prize, Barragán is an emblematic figure who contributed to Latin America's modern movement with his minimalist spiritual architecture.

Born in Guadalajara in 1902, Barragán studied civil engineering before embarking on a life-changing trip to Europe in 1924. His European travels introduced him to avant-garde architecture, which was burgeoning with the Bauhaus in Germany and around Le Corbusier in France. He also visited the influential 1925 Decorative Arts Exposition

"Any work of architecture which does not express serenity is a mistake."
Luis Barragán

in Paris, one of the first monumental displays of both decorative art deco and radical modernism. He was exposed to some of the most progressive architectural works of the time; he saw Le Corbusier's L'Esprit Nouveau Pavilion and Konstantin Melnikov's constructivist Soviet Pavilion. He also met Ferdinand Bac, a prolific landscape architect and writer whose work was

exhibited at the exposition. Having made the most significant impression of all on the young Mexican architect, Bac was even mentioned by Barragán in his 1980 acceptance speech for the Pritzker Architecture Prize.

European avant-garde was not the only influence on Barragán during his formative years. In Europe, he also saw traditional Mediterranean architecture, visiting Alhambra in Spain and other ▷

CASA GILARDI

Location: Mexico City, Mexico
Completion date: 1955

The façades of Casa Gilardi are unornamented—the windows have no sills and the whole presents a series of geometric forms. Characteristic of Barragán's work is his use of bright pink to create feature walls— a theme he continues on the inside. And also the position of the pink blossom tree is no accident.

Upon his return to Guadalajara in 1926, Barragán began the first phase of his architectural production, which spans, 1927 to 1936. During this period, he was still strongly influenced by Spanish colonial architecture with roots in his Mexican heritage. In 1936, he began to adopt a rational and functionalist style, designing a number of houses and apartment buildings, such as the 1936 Duplex in the Colonia Hipódromo and the 1939 Four Painters' Studios on Plaza Melchor Ocampo.

Moorish monuments in North Africa. His interest in ancient architecture was enriched by his memories of the landscape and vernacular ranch architecture of his native land. This unique mix of influences created a highly sensitive and spiritual architect, who became a true pioneer of Latin American modernism.

"... architects should design gardens to be used, as much as the houses they build." *Luis Barragán*

LUIS BARRAGÁN   CASA GILARDI

Location: Mexico City, Mexico
Completion date: 1952

Barragán had a fascination with light and the ways in which it could alter the atmosphere or appearance of a room. In Casa Galvez, he made features of transparent walls and screens and made much use of natural light, but also introduced artificial sources. The pink, in various shades, continues to the exterior of the building, in characteristic Barragán style.

But it was during the 1940s that Barragán arrived at the height of his own original style, the culmination of all of these influences. His own house, built between 1947 and 1948 in the Tacubaya district of Mexico City—and today under UNESCO protection—is emblematic of his signature style. Here, tradition meets modernity and modesty meets generosity. Barragán's house is the celebration of emptiness, silence, minimalism, light, color, and general poesy of architectural form. While the street façade is imposing and austere, the house opens toward a private garden in the rear and toward the sky on its roof terrace. Plain, unornamented walls create a place of peace, symbolically frozen in time. He also used a bright Mexican pink in the home, a color that became his signature in many projects to follow. Traditional wooden furniture sits around minimalist, custom-made designs that include a striking wooden staircase. At the same time, Barragán designed   ▷

CASA GALVEZ

colors of the modernist movement. In 1967, he created one of his best-known works, the Cuadra San Cristóbal equestrian estate. Built for the Egerstrom family, the Los Clubes complex in the suburbs of Mexico City includes stables, a house, and a pool, all done in a bright palette of pink, violet, and orange. The architect created a serene architectural landscape, a minimalist sculptural celebration of elementary forms and senses that has attracted the public since its inception. Famous photographer René Burri took photos here, and Louis Vuitton shot an advertising campaign within the space in 2016.

His color palette also holds a strong presence in his last residential project of 1977, the Gilardi House in Mexico City. In this project, colors become an essential quality of the architecture itself, creating a luminescent work of art. The Gilardi House showcases the architect's original and dramatic use of light, both

several houses within an experimental residential subdivision in the southern part of Mexico City. The rocky terrain, known as El Pedregal, was bought by Luis Barragán and his friend José Alberto Bustamante in 1945 and became a playground for the Mexican modernist movement. The harsh landscape had been considered uninhabitable since pre-Hispanic times, after the eruption of the nearby Xitle volcano. Barragán built several houses there, some of them in collaboration with Max Cetto. The most remarkable project was the Prieto López House. Built between 1947 and 1951, it was recently restored to its original modernist glory. El Pedregal was a laboratory of Mexican modernism, where young architectural talents followed Barragán and Cetto to build steel and glass houses in the dramatic volcanic landscape through the late 1960s.

During the 1950s and 1960s, Barragán also built several public projects. His Torres de Satélite in Mexico City, built in 1958 in collaboration with sculptor Mathias Goeritz, became a symbol of modern Mexico City. The striking monumental towers in the middle of the highway pay tribute to the geometry and

natural and artificial. His preference for hidden light sources gives the interior a particularly subtle and lyrical atmosphere—a true contribution from Barragán to the world of modern architecture.

The work of the Mexican master architect also influenced work of contemporary artists in very controversial ways. While conceptual artist Jill Magid created a diamond ring from the architect's real ash, his signature pink color was the main feature of a satirical

A unique mix of influences created a highly sensitive and spiritual architect, who became a true pioneer of Latin American modernism.

political statement of Mexican firm Estudio 3.14. The studio designed an utopian vision of Donald Trump's planned wall between Mexico and USA in the style of the famous architect. His legacy is still alive.   （STE）

CUADRA SAN CRISTOBAL

Location: Mexico City, Mexico
Completion date: 1968

At Cuadra San Cristobal, Barragán
landscapes the estate's vast
outdoor spaces using a series of
walls in bold, flat colors—his
trademark pink, but also rusty red
and mauve. The colors of the walls
are reflected in a "water mirror,"
into which a fountain spills. The
combined effect of these elements
is to create a tremendous air of
serenity.

The Labyrinth Home

Architect: Xavier Corbero
Location: Barcelona, Spain
Completion date: 1969 to present

There is poetry as well as a surreal eccentricity in Xavier Corbero's sculptural work, set within his incredible home for the last half century.

fig. a

fig. a: A beautifully crafted spiral staircase, in which the walls are cut to mirror the steps, has the effect of an optical illusion.

fig. b & c: Dominating the design inside and out is the arch, seen whole or in part, stacked one on top of another and in rows.

The estate of Spanish artist and sculptor Xavier Corbero is no less a labyrinth than the ancient run of tunnels and caves in the same location outside of Barcelona. This development has been ongoing for half a century and will doubtless continue for years to come. Amounting to some 5,000 square meters today—much of it underground—the complex serves as the artist's home, office, and studio space, as well as a museum for his work.

At the heart of Corbero's home stands a sculptural six-story atrium—a huge concrete column housed in a hexagonal glass case. All the way up, the structure is pierced with arches that allow light to flow into its core and into the rooms beyond. The effect is that of a kaleidoscope, the light dancing in ever-changing patterns as the sun moves across the sky. At the very top, the walls are planted with trailing plants that dangle into the void, casting shadows of their own.

Corbero works exclusively with concrete, glass, and wood. He favors the honesty of these materials and enjoys playing with their varied textures and the ways in which they complement one another. At an extreme level, there are rooms whose surfaces—walls, floor, and ceiling—are bare concrete; or rooms in which the ceilings, walls, and/or floors are clad in rough timbers. Elsewhere, concrete surfaces are highly polished or whitewashed to create a different effect altogether.

The growth of Corbero's creation over the decades has been organic, so he simply adds each new structure at whim. There are sliding walls and there are doors in floors—you never quite know where a staircase will lead you. Perhaps it is this that gives the place its surreal, maze-like atmosphere. That, and the prolific use of the arch—it is a dominant feature of the façade and serves as windows, doorways, and niches throughout the building. As you pass from one space to the next, you could be forgiven for feeling that—much like the atrium at the heart of the building—you are simply going around in circles. (SOU)

fig. b   fig. c (opposite page)

At the heart of Corbero's home stands a sculptural six-story atrium—a huge concrete column housed in a hexagonal glass case.

fig. d (opposite page)   fig. e

fig. d & e: The atrium
at the heart of the
house acts as a well
of light, casting
magical shadows
across the building's
interior spaces.

fig. f: Corbero
delights in the
juxtaposition of
unlikely materials
and objects. Here,
late art deco
furniture stands
in a room entirely
made of concrete.

fig. g: Looking up
toward the top of the
central atrium, its
upper levels drip in
vegetation.

fig. f   fig. g (following double page)

fig. h

fig. h: An exquisite chinoiserie screen mirrors the glazed hexagonal frame of the central atrium.

fig. i: Recent acquisitions await their final destination within the vast complex; among them, six Austrian chairs dating from 1820.

fig. j: No matter where you wander in this maze-like complex, you inevitably stumble across a total unique setting.

fig. k: This room is part studio, part gallery space. The lines are often blurred between the functions of a given space.

fig. i

XAVIER CORBERO   THE LABYRINTH HOME

fig. j   fig. k (following double page)

Corbero works exclusively with concrete, glass, and wood—He favors the honesty of these materials and enjoys playing with their varied textures and the ways in which they complement one another.

297

INDEX

Mirman House Arcadia by Buff,
Straub, and Hensman,
pp. 56–59

INSIDE *UTOPIA*

Visionary Interiors and
Futuristic Homes

This book was conceived, edited,
and designed by GESTALTEN.

Edited by ADAM ŠTĚCH, SALLY FULS, and ROBERT KLANTEN

Preface by SALLY FULS and ROBERT KLANTEN
Introduction by ADAM ŠTĚCH

Projects written by ANNA SOUTHGATE (SOU),
TIM ABRAHAMS (ABR), and ADAM ŠTĚCH (STE)
Portraits written by ADAM ŠTĚCH

Editorial management by MARIA-ELISABETH NIEBIUS

Copy-editing by RACHEL SAMPSON
Proofreading by FELIX LENNERT

Design and layout by JEANNINE MOSER
Creative direction of design by LUDWIG WENDT
Typeface: Fugue by RADIM PEŠKO

Cover photography by JULIUS SHULMAN, J. Paul Getty Trust. Getty
Research Institute, Los Angeles
Back cover photography by CARLO BAVAGNOLI/The LIFE Picture
Collection/Getty Images

Printed by OFFSETDRUCKEREI GRAMMLICH, Pliezhausen
Made in Germany

Published by GESTALTEN, Berlin 2017
ISBN 978-3-89955-696-4